D1505265

A HANDBOOK OF HERESIES

A HANDBOOK OF HERESIES

By

M. L. COZENS

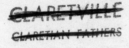
NEW YORK
SHEED & WARD
1947

FIRST PUBLISHED 1928
BY SHEED AND WARD, INC.
63 FIFTH AVENUE
NEW YORK, 3
REPRINTED 1947

NIHIL OBSTAT:
    GEORGIUS D. SMITH, S.T.D.
        CENSOR DEPUTATUS

IMPRIMATUR: EDM: CAN: SURMONT
    VIC. GEN.

WESTMONASTERII, DIE 4 JUNII 1928

1550

PRINTED IN GREAT BRITAIN

CONTENTS

INTRODUCTION

THE Revelation of God came to the world through the Hebrews, a people unused to abstract speculation, their very language too bald for Philosophy, so that Theology had to take the language of poetry, concrete images taking the place of definitions or syllogisms. These characteristics, whilst they prevented very great development of doctrine, were a safeguard against its perversion. When in the fullness of time Christ brought that complete Revelation of which Judaism was but the prologue, it was to the Hebrews that He spoke. He gave them His whole teaching—but in their own tongue, their own forms, not only of speech but of thought.

Yet His Church was to be no longer the Jewish Church, but the Catholic Church. His Revelation was to all mankind and was to be received and assimilated not by the practical ethical Hebrew only, but by the subtle-minded Greek, by the Eastern mystic, and by the childlike, untrained mind of far-off Goth and Barbarian.

When on the day of Pentecost the Holy Ghost descended upon that little band which Christ had formed and trained, they went forth to bring all minds into captivity to the truth; and these were not minds empty, waiting passively for the truth, but minds already active, with ideas, theories, and habits of thought of their own.

Into minds thus preoccupied the Christian Faith was to enter—to seize and act upon and mould them, and, within certain very rigid limits, to be reacted upon by them.

When Revelation took its rightful place as Ruler and Judge, then all of natural truth or mental power that a man had was enriched and crowned by it; all that was false or imperfect being abolished or rejected.

The Faith itself being more clearly set forth, more deeply penetrated, as the minds of men were brought to bear upon it, gave forth all its strength, light, and sweetness. That way lay development—a process which began the first moment a Christian meditated on Christ's teaching, and it shall not cease as long as one of the Faithful remains to keep the Faith.

But whenever Faith came to a mind not prepared to give it the first and ruling place, but determined to judge and test it by its own prepossessions, its own prejudices —then the truth became perverted, one-sided: and so were born heresies: so began the first heresy: so will heresies arise until Christ returns and Faith ends in Vision.

Well might the Apostles have quailed at the task before them. Simple Palestinian Jews, how should they commend their faith to the whole Gentile world, a world whose thought was so alien from their own? But their Risen Master had promised that the Holy Ghost should bring to their minds all things whatsoever He had told them.

In this knowledge, with this strength, they went forward knowing that whatever their personal weakness, however limited their individual knowledge or capacity, their mission could not fail, for He who had sent them had promised that the gates of hell should not prevail against them and that He would be with them even to the consummation of the world.

I. THE JUDAIC HERESY

THE Jews in Palestine who were converted by the Apostles at Pentecost, and in the years immediately following, were converted with all their Jewish traditions and prejudices. From earliest childhood they had been surrounded by every influence which could impress upon them the greatness of their privileges as members of the Chosen Race.

They were proud of their descent from Abraham, the Father of all the Faithful, in whose seed all the Nations should be blessed; proud of their fidelity to the Mosaic Law, which marked them out as a peculiar people, proud of their glorious temple and of the memory of that earlier temple in which, as the *Shekinah*, the glory of the Lord visibly dwelt. Every sabbath solemnity, every family festival in which social and religious life were most strongly and indestructibly blended; above all, each yearly Pasch, with its solemn commemoration of their great deliverance and of their founding as a Nation, strengthened this pride until it was enwoven into every fibre of their being.

Even when they had received the Faith and had accepted Christ, they thought of Him primarily as their own expected Messiah. True, they knew that He was not only Messiah but Lord, the God of Gentile as well as Jew, whose Church throughout the World Malachi had foretold; yet it seemed to them that surely the Gentiles could not be accepted straight from Heathendom; surely, if Judaism had been a preparation for Christianity, then the Gentile converts must go individually through that preparation which the whole Jewish race had undergone, and so be led through Moses to Christ. At least those who refused this discipline would remain in a lower state than those who submitted, so that in Christ's Church there would be two degrees—the Jews, and with them those who obeyed the Law of Moses, as the *élite*, the perfect Christians; below them those who, believing in Christ and admitted to baptism, declined to bear the yoke of the Law, and were an outer circle, saved indeed and part of the Church, but less privileged, less holy than the Mosaic *élite*. Even the Apostles themselves had not realised how completely Christ's Death on the Cross had broken down the barrier between Jew and Gentile, so that it needed a special revelation in vision to prepare St. Peter to admit Cornelius.

Where even the Apostles were slow to understand, little wonder that their converts found it still more difficult, and so from the first many among them took a certain scandal.

Meanwhile, outside Palestine, Christianity was spreading rapidly by means of the Dispersion. On the day of Pentecost we read "there were dwelling at Jerusalem Jews, devout men out of every nation under heaven." These men were staying in Jerusalem for Pentecost as Catholics now go up to Rome for Easter. They were the descendants of Jews who had been taken prisoners in war or who had left Palestine in search of gain, for then, as now, the Jews were a commercial and widely scattered people. In all the cities of Asia Minor and round the Mediterranean coast, they were a privileged class. Living among Greek-speaking people, to many of them the sacred Hebrew tongue was no longer familiar—so that a Greek translation of the Holy Scriptures had been made for use in their synagogues.

This translation was one of the ways by which the Gentile world was prepared for Christianity. So great a debt did the Church owe to it that an opinion was long current to the effect that the translators as well as the original authors of it, were inspired.

To the Jewish synagogues came many of the more spiritually-minded Gentiles. Some, willing to bear the whole burden of the Mosaic Law, if thereby they might be certain of a share in the God of Moses, were circumcised and so became full proselytes of righteousness. Others, unwilling to undertake so great a burden, yet found in the synagogue a doctrine of the Unity of God more clearly and certainly taught than in their highest philosophies, the highest ethical teaching, and with it, as Revealed truth, that doctrine which Philosophy doubted or denied, the Creation of the world, and the Love and care of the Creator for His creatures.

Here were, indeed, fields white for the harvest. These Jews held fast the Faith of Israel in the One Creator and the coming Redeemer, yet were less dominated by a narrow nationalism, less imbued with hatred or contempt for all that was not Jewish, than were the Jews of Palestine. Add to this that they were among Gentiles of good will, and were prepared by prayer and thought for further Revelation from God, and it can be seen how the Gospel could take root and flourish as it could not do either in tradition-bound Judea or in unprepared heathendom.

By the conversion of Saul of Tarsus to the Faith God provided the most fitting instrument for the work to be done, first in the synagogues and among the "God-fearers," as their Gentile fringe was called, and then, through them, among the heathens around them.

Born of a family settled at Tarsus in Cilicia and of sufficient importance to be "citizens" of Rome, Saul must have had opportunity in youth to contrast his position as a son of Israel and worshipper of the one Lord, with that of the devotees of the various barbarian and degenerate Greek cults around him. Being sent while still young to study at Jerusalem, he sat at the feet of the celebrated Hebrew teacher and theologian Gamaliel.

Here his racial pride was yet more strengthened. He imbibed the fiercest hatred of all enemies of the Jewish race or faith. Christianity to him appeared a treachery and heresy of the worst kind, and he threw himself with ardour into the work of repressing it. On the way from Jerusalem to Damascus he was converted by a vision of the Risen and Glorified Christ, and Saul the persecutor became Paul the Apostle.

From the first he realised with especial keenness the mystery concerning which he was to write so eloquently. The mystery of the incorporation of Jew and Gentile, Greek and Barbarian into the One Mystical Body of Christ.

When the news of the spreading of the Gospel among the Gentiles of Antioch reached Jerusalem, some of the more rigid of the Jewish Christians hastened thither, without any authority or mission from the twelve, and began to trouble the new converts, persuading them that circumcision, in addition to Christian baptism, was necessary for salvation. Paul, therefore, fearing lest his work should be ruined, and the spread of the Gospel hindered, went up with Barnabas to Jerusalem to confer with the Palestinian Church.

The Faithful at Jerusalem were gathered together with Peter and James, and when Paul had told them of God's mercies, shown in the conversion of Gentiles at his preaching, Peter arose and recalled to them all how he himself had received Gentiles into the Church, and how the Holy Ghost was given openly and miraculously even before baptism. Peter bade them pause before laying upon Gentile shoulders that yoke of the

Law which they, although Jews, had been unable to bear rightly, and James, assenting to Peter's decision, ordered that word should be sent to all the brethren of the Dispersion, that they should not trouble the Gentile converts, who should henceforth be required to keep only three points of the Old Law: to abstain from fornication, from things strangled, and from blood.

Most significant is the form in which this decree is set forth: "It seemeth good to the Holy Ghost and to us"; so strong was the conviction of the teaching Church, even in her infancy, that Christ's promise was literally fulfilled—that, when she spoke, the words were the words of God.

Nevertheless, some of the Jewish Christians refused to accept the decision of the Council and, recognising Paul as the great champion of Christian freedom and of the Gentile incorporation in Christ, looked upon him as their chief enemy. Henceforward we find them following Paul in his journeys, sowing dissensions among his followers, and trying everywhere to undermine his authority and to destroy his influence.

After the flight of the Palestinian Christians to Pella, two years before the destruction of Jerusalem, the Hebrews became more and more alienated from the rest of the Church. Thus while the Church pursued her course with increasing success through the nations, her divine truths being more deeply comprehended and more implicitly taught, the poor remnant of the first Christian Church turned more and more resolutely toward the past and away from the promise of the future.

They mourned the destruction of Jerusalem and did not dream that Rome, which was to them the Heathen Oppressor and the Mother of all abominations, would become another Holy City from which the Word of the Lord should go forth to the ends of the earth. They shut heart and mind against all expansion, all development. Gradually those truths of Revelation most foreign to Jewish thought faded from their minds. Parties were formed among them, with tenets varying in proportion as Christian or Jewish sentiment held greater sway in the minds of their members.

On the extreme right a party held nearly the whole Christian Faith but combined with it the rigid practice of the Jewish Law, thereby, tacitly at least, denying one point of faith—namely, that all the Old Law was fulfilled in Christ—so that dying in Him it bound no longer: Christians were free from it. At the other extreme was a party which rejected all the Gospels except a mutilated version of St. Matthew, denied the Virgin Birth, together with the Divine Nature of Christ, and regarded St. Paul as an enemy and corrupter of the Gospel.

Some, again, mixed with such fragments of Christian teaching as they retained scraps borrowed from Essenism, that strange off-shoot of Judaism which rejected sacrifice, forbade marriage, and taught a most un-Jewish contempt for the body.

So, while the light of Faith spread from land to land throughout the world, in that land where it first arose it faded, until by the fifth century the Hebrew Church existed no more.

II. THE GENTILE CONVERTS

MEANWHILE outside the confines of Palestine the Church spread from the East to Rome, from Rome throughout the Western World, so that by A.D. 200 Tertullian could write: "Many of the most distant Moors, all the Spains and the various nations of the Gauls and of the Britons, places unpenetrated by the Romans, are yet subject to Christ. Germans, Dacians and Scythians . . . in all these places the name of Christ has already come and reigned."

The triumphs of the Church can only be grasped when we realise something of the welter of ideas into which she came; the tumult in which she had to make her voice heard—for she spoke not in the stillness of a world hushed and waiting for her message, but in a very Babel of conflicting voices.

Rome had conquered the greater part of the known world. It was a world Roman in government, and Greek, at least superficially, in culture; and in its greater part the Graeco-Roman civilisation was but a thin crust, beneath which ancient superstition, folk-lore, and strange barbarian cults mingled and battled.

In the cities, at least, the main elements were: First, Roman, the polytheistic state religion; secondly, the Mystery Cults; thirdly, Philosophy; and fourthly, Hellenic Judaism.

THE ROMAN STATE RELIGION.

This was a mixed mythology. Originally it contained scarcely personified natural forces and civic qualities; then, as the Romans became Hellenised, their gods adopted the more definite personalities and poetic qualities of the Pantheons. In this way what they gained in beauty they lost in dignity and morality, getting from the Greeks qualities of lust and cruelty which made them as base as the basest of their worshippers.

Their worship was purely ritualistic, non-dogmatic, non-moral and non-mystical. Whilst no educated person could take it literally, yet it stood as an embodiment of the real enemy of God's Church, that is for the Supremacy of the State in all things. It was shot through and through with Imperialism and Emperor-worship. So undogmatic was it, that any and every national cult could find a place in it—if only Rome and Caesar might be the chief, or at least the immediate, object of worship.

From this source could come no *intellectual* heresy, yet the spirit of that old Caesar-worship was the nursing mother of many a heresy during the Church's life.

THE MYSTERY RELIGIONS.

While the State religion could offer nothing to the hungry souls of men, there persisted the deep craving for something greater and higher than the world could offer. To all men, but especially to the *best* and the *worst*, comes a desire to penetrate beyond this outward seeming, to a fuller, higher life—a "rebirth."

Both the idealist, striving to pierce through the shadows of sense to the one absolute reality, and the sensualist, sated and sick with the reaction from excess, craved something above themselves by which they might be delivered.

This cry of humanity, to which neither State Polytheism nor Philosophy responded, the Mystery Cults attempted to answer. These Cults, mostly Nature myths, came from the East or from Egypt, and promised to their initiates deliverance from sin and death through a Revelation and a Rebirth.

What these Cults promised the Church actually gave. She offered the sinner the laver of Regeneration wherein his sin might be cleansed, the death and burial of the old man—an entrance into the liberty of the children of God. She bade the souls athirst for union with God— to come to the Word made flesh, to eat His flesh and drink His blood, that so they might become one with Him. She made her children, through the Sacraments, partakers of the Divine Nature, and promised them beyond this life entrance into those things "which eye hath not seen nor ear heard."

Among the Gentiles it would be precisely those drawn to the Mystery Cults who would be most attracted to the Church; and let us repeat once more—they, not less than the converts from Judaism, came to the Church not with empty minds but with minds full of their own conceptions and misconceptions, which the Truth had to judge—to sift, cast out, correct, or complete.

So we find that while Paul had so often, among the Jews, to fight the notion of Salvation by legal good works, in writing to his *Gentile* converts he had to be equally insistent upon the necessity for good works in the regenerate.

Many of the converts were prone to imagine that to be Reborn was enough—to them, as to later heretics, emotion, ecstasy, or "spiritual experience," was all that mattered, and they despised the commandments as savouring of that "old law" or "old man" from which their baptism had freed them. So that we find Paul writing to his beloved converts, exhorting them to find in the remembrance of their baptism the motive for a life of good works—meet fruit of the new life-principle within them. In writing to the Corinthians he

B

corrects the abuse in their celebrations of the Eucharist and in that we seem to catch a hint of fear lest the sexual abuses familiar to the worshippers of Asiatic deities should creep into the Sanctuary and pollute the Mysteries of their Redemption.

Once more the issue was determined by the attitude of each mind to the Faith. Those who made the Act of Faith more sincerely gave up every thought not in accordance therewith, whilst those who sought in the Church their own highest ideals, apart from God's revelation, fell away into one or other of those bewildering nightmarish heresies which haunted the outskirts of Christianity during the end of the first and the whole of the second century.

THE PHILOSOPHERS.

"Hear, O Israel, the Lord thy God. The Lord He is One."

"In the beginning God created the heavens and the earth."

These are the two great revealed doctrines of Judaism.

To the first some of the great Thinkers of other races had arrived, though slowly and with difficulty, by reason; but to the second no Greek or Asiatic had come. Israel alone knew—and she not by reason, but by revelation—that the One—the Ineffable—the Infinite, was also the Creator, the Ruler, the Judge. The Greek, in proportion as he realised the Holiness and Immutability of God, shrank from bringing Him into contact with changing creatures, above all with Matter, which to the Greek mind stood for all that is opposed to Goodness and Being, not simply the contrary of Spirit but its contradictory.

The Church bade him believe—first, that all things,

spirit and matter alike, were created by God, approved and loved by Him in varying degrees according to their varying degrees of being; secondly, more astonishing still, that He had assumed into the Unity of the Second Person of the Godhead, not only the lowest order of spiritual being, the human soul, but a material body— "The Word was made Flesh."

Faced with this terrific dogma, the Greek-trained mind, once it made the Act of Faith, began that sublime meditation which brought all Philosophy to illumine and develop the truths of Faith; that unending meditation, of which all the definitions of Councils are points, all the writings of the Fathers preludes.

This is the crowning point, the highest glory of reason, to be raised above itself—to work freely in regions of which, unaided, it could not dream, much less reach and explore.

III. GNOSTICISM

IT has been held by many theologians that the great test of Angelic virtue, the issue of which decided the eternal fate of each of the Celestial host, was the Vision of the Incarnate God. Those spirits who, bowing their glorious intelligences, adored a nature so inferior to their own yet hypostatically united to the eternal Word, were by that humiliation exalted for ever—even to the participation of that Word's Divine Nature. They who, on the contrary, refused—sank by their refusal into eternal ruin. So it was again now. Christ is ever that stone on which they who stumble shall be broken. As in the beginning of God's creation this mystery was the point at issue between the obedient and disobedient angels, so in the beginning of God's new Creation—the Church. Those who hold fast to the great declaration of St. John—"The Word was God . . . and the Word was made flesh"—were safeguarded against all the manifold forms of error, while those who refused to sacrifice old forms of thought and old prejudices—including their contempt for matter—to the Divine revelation of God Incarnate, fell into one or other fantastic heresy.

A chameleon-like group of these heresies is known to us to-day as Gnosticism. Gnosticism springs from tendencies visible even in Apostolic times, but only appearing as a clearly definable heresy or group of heresies about the middle of the second century. During the three hundred years or so in which we see it opposing the Church of God, setting its pride of knowledge against the humility of faith, we find it taking a bewildering variety of shapes. To describe it is like trying to describe the ever-changing pattern within a revolving

20

kaleidoscope. Each teacher reforms it, or adds some startling variation of his own.

All, however, agree in their contempt for matter, and hence deny any true Incarnation. Between the Supreme Unchanging God and His creation, they postulate many emanations in a descending scale until we reach a being so far inferior as to be capable of contact with matter. This being, whom some Gnostics held to be not only less good but actually evil, created this material universe, imprisoning therein certain sparks of good or spirit coming from either God or some higher emanation nearer the supreme Good. It was to deliver this divine spark or sparks that they thought the Redeemer had come, but since they held matter altogether evil, He did not actually assume it but only some phantom thereof, or at most a body like to an earthly body but of heavenly immaterial origin.

If any of them, as the Valentinians, admit a real humanity in Jesus, then they anticipate Nestorius, and hold only an accidental link between the Divine Word and that human element which was His instrument of Redemption. Nearly always, also, they depreciate the Old Testament, and in Marcion this depreciation becomes an important part of his teaching, since to him the Old Testament was the Revelation and Law of that inferior evil principle, the Demiurge, who created matter and from whom Christ, whose revelation was the Gospel, came to deliver His redeemed. With the exception of Marcion, who taught deliverance from the power of the Demiurge by an exaggerated asceticism, the Gnostics taught salvation not by faith and love but by speculative knowledge or in later more degraded development by magical rites, and they constantly taunt the Catholics with contented ignorance, since *they* teach the way of simple faith.

Manacheism, in which the youthful mind of the great Augustine was for long entangled, was but a later development from the same principles, and throughout the Middle Ages we see it reappearing sporadically like a pestilence.

The Albigenses, whom many people imagine as precursors of Evangelical Pietism, taught a peculiarly poisonous, because peculiarly practical, variant of the same heresy. Holding matter, and the life of the senses bound up with matter, to be altogether evil, they considered marriage and procreation essentially wrong and, therefore, abortion and sometimes suicide commendable: nor in extreme cases did they hesitate to allow a certain practical assistance from their initiates to a neophyte who shrank at the last moment from this supremely logical conclusion.

The doctrine of the essentially evil nature of the body and its instincts has always led, according to the character of those receiving it, to exactly opposite ethical conclusions. The lower sort reasoned that since the body was irredeemable its baser cravings might be freely indulged, that the soul being no longer tormented by its unappeased clamours might seek God in peace; on the other hand those less carnal-minded taught a harsh and unbending asceticism, which, aiming at extirpating natural instincts, too often broke down in practice and ended in licence equal to that of the former party.

IV. MONTANISM

In reading the history of the infant Church in the New Testament, we are struck by the frequency of extraordinary external manifestations accompanying the reception of the Holy Ghost and His interior gifts.

Not to linger on the familiar story of Pentecost with its rushing wind, its tongues of fire and gift of tongues, we find that when Cornelius the Centurion and his companions, yet unbaptised, heard St. Peter's testimony to the Resurrection of Christ, the Holy Ghost fell upon them and they also spoke with tongues.

In the early days of the Church at Corinth, so plentifully were many of the faithful endowed with these marvellous gifts, that their exercise seemed likely to hinder rather than promote the spiritual welfare of the whole body, so that St. Paul, in writing his first epistle to the Corinthians, has to correct the disorder occasioned by the Corinthians' want of temperance and discipline in spiritual things. When they met together for worship, some rapt in the Spirit would utter unintelligible sounds, others less absorbed would tell aloud the wonders God was working in them or revealing to them. St. Paul, while acknowledging the divine source of these extraordinary favours, yet exhorts his converts to value above them the gifts of interior sanctity—and to regulate their use of the more extraordinary gifts as should be most for the edification of the whole Church.

Nor was the risk of irreverence or scandal the only or the greatest danger. These manifestations, or mystical phenomena, as they were afterwards called, were far more easily counterfeited by Satan than are the more ordinary workings of the Holy Ghost, and so souls, themselves misled, might lead others astray to spiritual ruin.

The only safeguard was humility and obedience. When the gift was genuine it was accompanied always by respect for the regular and authorised channels of spiritual truth and grace, whilst those who resisted authority proved themselves to be led not by the Spirit of Peace and Truth, but by that rebel spirit whose motto is "I will not serve."

As time went on the prayer and worship of the Church under the guidance of the Holy Ghost formed and flowed in two definite channels. The public worship of the Church crystallised into the Liturgy, in which the needs and aspirations of the whole Church and of each member of it are summed up in words which every one of the faithful can make his own, and under the guardianship of the same spirit Bishops taught and theologians developed those dogmatic truths which the Liturgy presupposes and serves. (In this connection it is interesting to note how St. Paul brings back the Corinthians from the consideration of private revelation and prophecy to the dogmatic truths, when, after giving very definite instructions on the use of tongues and prophecy, he immediately returns to the Death and Resurrection of Christ.)

The extraordinary manifestations of God's power in prayer and worship were withdrawn more and more from public gaze, while remaining ever a part of the life and worship of Christ's Mystical Body, as may be seen in the lives of countless saints and mystics down through the ages. Yet these gifts are held and exercised always under the authority and guidance of the teaching Church, to whom it always belongs to test the spirits.

It was the lack of submission to her guidance that was responsible for Montanism, a heresy which takes its name from Montanus, a Phrygian Christian, who about the third quarter of the second century began to show signs and wonders which to some seemed a revival of those attending the first days of the Church, while others feared, rightly as the issue proved, that they were rather due to diabolical possession.

Claiming to act under the immediate inspiration of the Holy Ghost, Montanus and his followers first preached a revival of penance and of primitive fervour. Gradually, however, they exalted themselves above the official hierarchy of the Church, and under the pretence of a new and personal revelation taught the immediate Second Advent and imposed new commandments forbidding remarriage to the widowed, and imposing on all rigorous fasting. At last their arrogance reached the blasphemous height of declaring that the Holy Ghost had descended upon Montanus and his followers in a higher and fuller manner than upon the Apostles at Pentecost, enabling him to teach things higher than they, nay, even than Christ Himself.

Both its emotional character and its severe asceticisms appealed especially to the more thorough-going and devout sex, so we are not surprised to find two women, Priscilla and Maximilla, foremost among Montanus' early following. One prophetess indeed declared that Christ had appeared to her under the form of a woman, and women as well as men appeared as officials in the revivalistic orgies before Montanistic altars.

Tertullian, the writer to whom the Latin Church owes so much, fell a victim to the heresy, and in his later work, *De Pudicitia*, between 217 and 222, attacks the Roman Pontiff with extreme bitterness because he refused to sanction the merciless rigorism which Montanism inculcated.

Like all heresies, Montanism caused in some minds a rebound to the opposite extreme.

Because the mystical character of St. John's gospel and its insistence on the work of the Paraclete make him the favourite evangelist of the Montanists, certain other Christians would have none of him and refuse accordingly to give Our Lord the Johannine title of the Word, or Logos, and are accordingly known as the Alogi.

V. SABELLIANISM

THE first confession of faith in the Godhead of Jesus Christ was brief and simple. "Thou art the Christ, the son of the living God," was St. Peter's declaration, and for many years no more detailed statement was asked for from any convert. "I believe . . . in Jesus Christ His only Son our Lord," recited the Roman neophyte at his baptism; it was the childhood of the Church. As Christian children to-day believe fully that Our Lord is God, without understanding or indeed enquiring into all that the belief implies and involves, so during the first age Christians worshipped and died for Christ, without discussing how Christ could be God and distinct from the Father, and yet not another God, but the One God alone.

At the end of the third century, however, a doctrine was mooted at Rome—brought probably from Asia, where Neotus had preached during the preceding decade a doctrine strongly resembling it—which tried to elucidate the problem by stating that Father and Son were but different aspects or conditions of the one being—God being Father when we consider Him as the Supreme Being who created the Universe, but Son as Revealed in Jesus Christ. It was the Father, they said, who by taking flesh of Mary became Son.

When such sayings of Our Lord as "The Father is greater than I," or "No man knoweth the Father save the Son," were quoted against them, they said that the Son was the Manhood, the Father the Godhead in Christ: and so, abandoning their first statement, that the Father had suffered—whence their name Patripassian—they now said that while the Son—that is the flesh or the man—suffered, the Father or Spirit compassionated

27

with Him. "Filius sic quidem patitur, pater vero compatitur."

This heresy, from its most noted exponent Sabellius, is known as Sabellianism. It was condemned by Pope Callistus, the same Pope whose mercy towards repentant sinners called forth the bitter invective of the rigorous Montanist Tertullian—and made little lasting impression in Rome; but in the East it flourished throughout the fourth and into the fifth century.

The rise of Arianism perhaps tended to push some souls into this, the opposite, heresy; for the blasphemous Arian attempt to separate the Father and the Son, led the more impatient, or less clearheaded, adorers of Christ to make the distinction between Him and the Father nominal only.

By the fourth century the heresy had developed in fresh directions. God in His own Nature, the Sabellians, or as they preferred to call themselves, Monarchists, claimed, was one person only. In His work as Creator He takes the name of Word. The Word is God as manifested in creation.

We seem to see here a reappearance of the old Philonic idea of the Logos, not as a distinct person, but either the idea of the Universe in the mind of God, or, the image of God in the Universe.

Now the Three Persons of the Christian Trinity, the Sabellians went on to explain, were not realities or relations in the Godhead, but merely relations of God to mankind. Revealing Himself in the old Law as Creator, He is the Father. In the New Law as Incarnate Redeemer, He is the Son. As the Paraclete, the guide of the Church, the sanctifier of souls, He is the Holy Ghost. In short the Sabellian would have been quite content to express himself in the terms of the Anglican Catechism. "First I learn to believe in

God the Father who hath made me and all the World; secondly in God the Son who hath redeemed me and all mankind; and thirdly in God the Holy Ghost who sanctifieth me and all the elect people of God."

Once the work of the Spirit was accomplished the triune personality, being but a threefold mask, would disappear and the one undifferentiated God would remain in His simplicity.

VI. ARIANISM

WHILE the rulers of the Church were still engaged in the struggle with Sabellianism, a new and far more formidable heresy appeared in Alexandria.

This city, which had long been as famous for its intellectual, as for its commercial, wealth and privileges, was the centre of a great Apologetic movement. There, where the Greek, the native Egyptian, and the Hebrew met and discoursed more freely than perhaps in any other place, their minds were open to receive the Gospel message if only it were presented in a manner capable of assimilation. To meet this opportunity, the Alexandrian Church founded its renowned Catechetical School. Here Catechumens were instructed—catechists trained, and the whole work of apologetics fostered amidst almost ideal conditions.

In the year 319, Alexander the Patriarch was presiding in person over some of the exercises, when one of the clerics present, Arius, brought forward a question concerning the sense in which the words "Son of God" were to be understood.

It is, of course, obvious that since all our language expresses concepts formed from things around us—no form of words, no idea even, can fully set forth the things of God, or can express the Divine Being who became Incarnate for us.

He Himself, however, whilst on earth, named Himself the Son of God, and St. John, inspired by the Holy Ghost, calls Him "The Word"—"In the beginning was the Word and the Word was with God and the Word was God." Both these names are necessary to a true, though still only analogous, idea of the relation of Our Lord to the Father. The first, "Son," declaring Him of the same Nature as the Father; the second, "Word," reminding us most forcibly of the utter spirituality of that Nature, and warning us from any gross or materialistic notion of the Divine Fatherhood or Sonship. Arius, however, brought forward only the first of these and asked—"If God the Son was begotten of the Father, does that not imply that the Father existed before Him."

Alexander, after much patient exhortation and argument, was forced to excommunicate Arius, who—having first put his heresy only as a difficulty or question—refused when corrected to accept the orthodox answer and, rather than own that there are necessarily mysteries in the Divine Nature far above our comprehension, denied the Divine Filiation in everything but name.

Since human sons must be less in age than those who beget them, he foolishly argued from humanity, living in time, to Him who *is* Eternity, concerning whom "before" and "after" are meaningless terms.

Forgetting that the essence of Sonship is the receiving from a Parent his own nature—transmitted to the son, and that since God's nature is Eternal and Unchangeable, the Son must be Eternal and Unchangeable as the Father, the heretic argued thus: "He is Son: therefore posterior to the Father; therefore not eternal. Since the Father is Eternal and the Son not, He is unlike the Father."

When confronted with the passages in Scripture which ascribe to Him Divine honour and Divine attributes, Arius and his followers, for soon the heretic gained a large following, owned that He was Son and Lord and even God, but said that He was all this, not necessarily and essentially but because the Father willed to make Him so. He was, they held, only a super-angelic being, the first and highest creature of God, in fact the only being directly created by God, the Father having brought

Him into being that by and through Him He might create the Universe. Because of His fidelity to God, God had caused Him to be exalted to share in the Divine prerogatives, and when Catholics urged that in that case —if His nature were mutable—it would have been possible for Him to commit sin, Arius at first did not shrink from owning the full consequences of his blasphemy, but said that it would have been possible.

To add to the horror of Catholics, Arius was not content with bringing forward these blasphemous novelties in academic circles, where their indecencies might have been veiled in technical language; and where minds accustomed to debate might have kept their balance amid the swirl of argument and counter-argument. He brought the subject under discussion out into the street and market-place, and made the Mystery of the Divine Generation the subject of popular songs or hymns. Soon an only half-Christianised populace were debating and even rudely jesting on doctrines which, theoretically at least, were only revealed to the convert after a long preparation and gradual training.

Excommunicated by Alexander, his Diocesan and Patriarch, Arius took refuge in Caesarea, where the bishop Eusebius protected him and allowed him to promulgate his heresy, himself adopting the same opinions more cautiously expressed.

Arius at first had not shrunk from any conclusion, however blasphemous, following from his premises, nor from the baldest statement of his principles. Now, taught by a group of worldly and cautious prelates who made his cause their own, he learned to disguise this worst of blasphemies beneath ambiguous terms. He withdrew the statement that the Son was by nature mutable—called Him the "Only begotten," meaning thereby "Only directly Created," and strove in letters

to Alexander and others to pose as a persecuted, misunderstood and innocent believer.

So great was the dispute engendered by Arius and
his friends—some bishops adopting his heresy, others
excommunicating him and his adherents, while others,
deceived by his use of orthodox terms, scarcely knew
which party to encourage—that the whole East was in
a ferment and it became necessary to convoke a council
of the whole Church.

This had been rendered possible by the conversion, or
semi-conversion, of the Emperor Constantine years before.
He, rashly interfering with the teachings of that Church
of which he was yet only a Catechumen, first wrote to
Alexander and Arius, treating the question as one about
subtleties and trifles, bidding them cease their disputes
and resume their former relations for the sake of the
peace of the Church.

This letter having, naturally, little effect, the Emperor
encouraged the wishes of the bishops concerned for a
General Council, and in 325 the famous Council of Nicæa
gathered together—the first of the great Ecumenical
Councils in which from time to time the Church has
defined her dogmas, condemned heresies, and regulated
her worship and discipline.

In this Council the first need was to find a term which
should act as a decisive test of a man's belief in the
Godhead of the Son. After much consideration the
word Homoousion was fixed on as being the only one
whose force the heretics could not evade or explain
away. This word which our English creed gives as
"Consubstantial or Of one substance with," was not
altogether pleasing even to some of the orthodox. At
this date the whole technical language of theology,
now the most fixed and exact in existence, was yet un-
developed and unfixed, and a few objected to speaking

c

of God's substance at all, lest they should seem to coun-
tenance a materialistic view of the Divine Nature. More
disliked the word because it had been used by some in
the previous century in a Sabellian sense—to deny the
distinct personality of the Son.

No other word, however, could be found to express
the essential union between the Father and the Son,
for every other word the Arians accepted, but in an
equivocal sense. They would deny that the Son was
a creature as other creatures—or in the number of the
creatures—or made in time, for they considered Him
a special Creation made before time. They would call
Him "Only Begotten," meaning "only directly created"
Son of God. They would call Him "Lord Creator,"
"First-born of all Creation," they even accepted "God
of God," meaning thereby "made God by God." This
word alone they could not say without renouncing their
heresy. To be of the one substance with the Father is
to be God substantially, essentially as the Father Himself
is—differing only in Personality—that is Relation, for
the Father begets, whilst the Son is begotten.

Faced with this unavoidable issue, the Arians who,
bear in mind, had first raised the discussion—who first
had gone beyond the Scriptures to be impious, now
decried any term not in Scripture used for pious guarding
of the Faith. Let us keep to the plain words of Scripture, they pleaded, having first shown by their evasions
that the words of Scripture were not so plain that beneath
their cover heresy could not be maintained.

In spite of these pathetic pleas for the rights of Holy
Writ, the Council accepted and defined the Homoousion
and insisted on its acceptance by all who claimed Catholic
communion. Arius was excommunicated afresh and the
Emperor insisted on the acceptance of the definitions and
findings of the Council as a duty not only to the Church

but also to the State, whose peace, he held, was compromised by obstinate heretics or schismatics.

The Emperor's wish for the peace of the Church, although, as we have seen, it greatly facilitated the work of the Council and the publishing of its decrees, had many unfortunate consequences. Some worldly bishops, among them Eusebius of Caesarea and his namesake of Nicomedia, signed the Creed of Nicæa—not in submission to the truth of God but to obey the will of the Emperor. Men of worldly character, they disliked dogmatic precision and wished for some comprehensive formula which men of all opinions could sign whilst understanding it in widely diverging senses. To these men the precise and exact faith of an Athanasius, and the obstinate heresy of Arius and his plain-spoken followers were equally distasteful.

"Respectable, tolerant, broadminded," would be their ideal of religion. They therefore brought forward, instead of the too-definite ineradicable Homoousion—of *one* substance, the vaguer term Homoiousion, i.e. of *like* substance. They sent letters far and wide couched in seemingly orthodox and fervent language—proclaiming their belief in Our Lord's divinity, ascribing to Him every divine prerogative, anathematising all who said He was created in time: in short, saying all the most orthodox could ask, *except* that they substituted their own Homoiousion for the Homoousion of Nicæa.

Many of the faithful, even many bishops in the West, misled by their artifices, accepted these statements, and since the whole controversy turned on the meaning of Greek phrases, very imperfectly understood in the Latin-speaking and Latin-thinking world, began to think that those who stood fast to the definitions and decrees of Nicæa were over-rigid precisians, more anxious about terminology than about fraternal charity.

Meanwhile these latter, foremost among them Athanasius, at first deacon and disciple of Alexander, Bishop of Alexandria, and afterwards his successor, refused to modify in any way their attitude. Steadfastly they refused to accept any statement not containing the Homoousion or to communicate with those who rejected it.

The case of the latitudinarian Eusebians has found defenders among the worldly-minded all through the ages, until it is summed up in the well-known sneer at the whole Christian world convulsed about a diphthong. How little they realised that on that one diphthong depended the whole Christian Faith.

VII. SEMI-ARIANISM

SOME Catholics, as we said above, unsuspiciously accepted the word "of like Substance"—they of course understood by it *exactly* like, i.e. identical. The opposite party accepted it in the opposite sense: "like" means somewhat resembling, as we say that a candle is *like* a star, and gradually there grew up a party who gave to the indefinite term a very definite interpretation of their own. They denied the consubstantiality of the Father and the Son; nevertheless they would not allow that the Son was created, but considered Him to be born of the Father, yet not God—something less than God, yet more than a creature, not of *one* but of *like* substance.

These Semi-Arian heretics, like the sneerers at the all-important diphthong, did not realise that between God's substance and all, even the highest, other substances, the distance is simply infinite. To be "like" God is to be utterly unlike Him: between even the highest Archangel and the lowest fungus there can be some relation of comparison. Between God, and all that is not God, there is no comparison possible.

Were there a being as far above Michael as Michael is above an earthworm, then a being as much greater again, and were this proportion repeated a thousand million times, yet the greatest of these magnified glories would be infinitely below the One Self-existence. There is no middle term possible: either Our Lord is God, Equal to—One with—the Father: or He is, however great, however exalted, our fellow-creature—our fellow-servant.

Against such a degradation of Our Lord and Saviour stands for ever the great cry of Nicæa, repeated each Sunday, "Deum de Deo, Lumen de Lumine, Consubstantialem Patri."

VIII. APOLLINARIANISM

ARIUS, in addition to his heresy concerning the *divine* nature of the Son, also taught an equally heretical view of His human nature. He took flesh, he said, and not soul. In Christ the place of the human soul was taken by the pre-existing Son.

Christ was, in this theory, a being compounded of a super-angelic spirit and a human body.

This latter heresy, which with Arius was something like a side issue, became the leading tenet of a man who is first known as one of Arius' foremost antagonists.

Apollinaris, Bishop of Laodicea, taught strongly the absolute Godhead of the Son and the true Deity of Christ; but in his anxiety to safeguard the oneness of Christ's Person, he sacrifices the reality and dignity of His humanity. Apollinaris seems here to have anticipated the modern philosophical error that "personality" equals "consciousness," for he argues that if we admit an intelligence in Christ other than the word, we thereby admit two personalities; but whereas modern Liberals say, "He had a human intelligence, therefore He was not God," Apollinaris said, "He was God, therefore He had not a human intelligence." When he first developed his thesis, about the year 360, in opposition to the teaching (over-lax in precisely the opposite direction) of the Bishop of the neighbouring See of Antioch, he said that in Christ the Word was the sole animating principle; but to avoid the crudity of attributing to the Word the lower activities of the human soul, he adopted the trichotomist theory of man's nature. That is to say, instead of holding, as he had done hitherto, that the human soul is the one principle of all human activity, he now taught that man was threefold, body, soul and spirit: and that while Christ had human flesh and that lower animal soul which was the principle of its sensitive movements—the rational soul, which knows and chooses, was wanting, its place being supplied by the Word.

This heresy, while it seemed to simplify the doctrine of the incarnation, did so by sacrificing its reality and value. It lowered both the Godhead and the Manhood: for while the humanity was not of the same nature as ours but mere brute flesh, the Godhead was made mutable since it became capable of the *successive* acts of a created intelligence.

These theories also emptied of all meaning those passages of the Gospels in which Christ prays to His Father—or which speak of His obedience, since only a free rational will can submit or obey. Christ's Divine Will, being one substantially with the Father's, cannot be submitted thereto.

As Apollinaris had so distinguished himself hitherto as a champion of the Church against Arius, his fellow bishops for some time treated him with leniency, hoping that his heresy was merely verbal, or at worst due to confusion of thought, and that once its dangerous nature was pointed out he would explain himself in an orthodox sense. However, he not only persisted in his errors, but having imbued others with the heresy, they promulgated it more and more plainly and defiantly. Several of the Fathers of the Church, notably St. Basil, attacked him; and in the year 377, Pope Damasus condemned his doctrine and deposed him and his follower, Timothy, from their sees. This heresy, like all others departing from the unity of faith, could not keep unity even with itself— some of the followers of Apollinaris taught that Christ had a sensitive human soul, but not a rational one—the Word supplying its place; others that nothing in Christ was Human save His flesh; others taught that even His flesh was not truly human, holding the extraordinary view that the Godhead itself was changed into literal flesh.

Other weird ideas—midway between, or admixture of these—were also held, so that the variety of heresies, seeming mutually destructive, attributed to the Apollinarians by writers of the following centuries, are so numerous as to seem incredible, had we not sad experience in these modern days of how numerous and how utterly diverse can be the spawn of any one error.

The orthodox bishops met the heresy by insisting upon, and more and more clearly developing, the relation between the Incarnation and the Redemption. The whole man had fallen in Adam—man's whole nature was wounded. Sin had affected not only the body and the sensitive powers, but also and principally the spiritual faculties—the intellect and will. If only the body was assumed by Christ, then only the body was healed by Him. The ruin wrought by the first Adam's misuse of Free-will could only be undone by the Free-will act of the new Adam, and unless Christ had a rational human soul, He was not capable of a free-will human act. They sum up at length their exposition in the well-known axiom, "Nothing is healed that is not assumed."

IX. NESTORIANISM

As by these definitions and condemnations the God-head of Our Lord and the reality of His Incarnation stood out more and more clearly before the minds of the faithful, certain consequences became apparent.

One of the most direct was the exaltation of Mary. Christ was very God. He was nevertheless her true son. Since God became her Son, she was Theotokos, God-bearer, Mother of God; and the title was freely used and gladly sung, particularly in many parts of the East. Already, for example, St. Ephrem the Syrian had praised her in language which in its exuberance of fervour vies with that of St. Alphonsus Liguori himself.

Imagine, then, the consternation when some time during 428 or 429, the newly-consecrated Bishop of Constantinople attacked the title Theotokos in the Cathedral pulpit of Constantinople, saying that Mary was indeed Mother of Christ but not Mother of God.

At once the new teaching was openly attacked by the clergy of Constantinople, and as soon as the news of the heresy spread, neighbouring bishops became alarmed. In explanation of his objection to the orthodox title, Nestorius was more and more plainly seen to be heretical on the doctrine of the Incarnation. Though claiming to adore One Son and One Christ in two natures, he so explained the union of those natures as to make it little more than a moral union of two distinct persons.

Cyril, Bishop of Alexandria, wrote warning all the monks of Egypt against this heresy, then wrote to Nestorius himself, and finally wrote to Celestine, then Pope, submitting both his own writings and the answers of Nestorius to the judgment of the Holy See. The Pope, having examined the documents, condemned the teaching

41

of Nestorius, ordered him to recant within ten days, and authorised Cyril to receive the recantation or in default thereof to condemn Nestorius and depose him from his See.

Nestorius, far from submitting, published his heresy more plainly and widely than ever. "The man Jesus," he said, "is the temple, the vesture of the Word . . . God did not die." "If Mary is called Mother of God, she is made a Goddess." Nor was the silly sneer lacking —to which Protestant controversialists have accustomed us to-day, "A mother cannot bear a Son older than herself."

Nestorius himself, unwilling to submit to Cyril, wished for a General Council. The Emperor favoured the idea, and the bishops began to gather from far and near. The Pope, glad to have the formal acquiescence of the East to the condemnation of Nestorius, which he had already pronounced, sent not only two Latin bishops, Arcadius and Projectus, but also Philip, a Roman priest, as his own special legate.

The Council was opened on the 22nd of June, although the Papal envoys and a large number of Nestorius' friends also had not yet arrived, and Nestorius was summoned to attend both to recant and also to account for his refusal to submit to Cyril as the representative of Celestine.

Nestorius, however, sent only contemptuous replies, although the summons was three times repeated. The Council therefore proceeded in his absence. Cyril's letter to Nestorius was read with the latter's heretical reply, and also the letter from the Pope authorising Cyril to depose Nestorius; Nestorius still refusing to plead in person, several fellow-bishops gave testimony of heresies uttered in their presence and finally the Council pronounced sentence: "Our Lord Jesus Christ who has been blasphemed by him has defined by this holy synod that the same Nestorius is excluded from all episcopal dignity and from every assembly of bishops."

When the Roman priest and bishops arrived on July 10 a further session began. Philip, after referring to the sentence of Celestine already accepted and promulgated by the Council, gave a further message from the Pope, which the assembled Fathers greeted with acclamation.

In all, the Council held seven sessions, and Nestorius and his followers were utterly condemned, together with Pelagius and other heretics. All the Ephesian populace received the decision of the Council with the utmost joy. Crowds surged through the streets bearing lights and joyfully acclaiming the honour of the Theotokos: "Thou, O Mother of God, hast destroyed the heresy."

That instinct which filled Ephesus with rejoicing multitudes was abundantly justified. The heresy of Nestorius, which seems chiefly an attack on the Mother, is a yet more deadly attack on her Son.

Nestorius held that in Jesus Christ there were not only two natures but two distinct beings. He was willing, indeed, to say there was but one person, but his other expressions make it abundantly clear that by person he meant something other than the Catholic meant by the same term. The Church teaches that God the Son was not united to an already existing being, but that Christ's human nature, when first created by God, was not given one moment's purely human existence. From the first moment, it existed, not as a single independent existing essence or nature, but as the human nature of the Word. It was *His* nature, not as our garments are our garments, but as our hearts are our hearts, united to His eternal Godhead with a union so close that the only analogy we can find is the union in man of soul and body.

"As the reasonable soul and flesh is one man, so God and man is one Christ."

Nestorius, however, thought of the human nature as the Word's human nature in the other—or accidental—sense. He called the Human Nature the vesture or temple of the Godhead, and made a very wide distinction between the acts of the human nature and the acts of the Divine person. In doing so he betrayed his erroneous use of the word person—since acts are the acts not of natures but of persons.

Likewise, mothers bring forth not natures but children, that is persons: so that to call Mary Mother of God is to affirm clearly and unmistakably the true doctrine of the Incarnation. Mary is literally and truly the Mother of Jesus, therefore He is true man. Jesus is true God, therefore she is Mother of God.

When the Council had finished its labours and its decrees and definitions had received the approval of Pope Sixtus III (St. Celestine having died during the sitting of the Council), the Emperor enforced the deposition of those whom it condemned, and after a brief struggle the heretics were driven out of the Church, and also out of the Roman Empire. Many fled into Persia, and the King of Persia was glad to find any means of antagonising the Persian Christians and those Christians who were under the authority of Pope and Emperor; for he always feared that union with the Roman Pontiff in religion might lead his Christian subjects to desire union with the Roman Empire in secular matters also. He therefore encouraged Nestorianism and allowed the heretics to obtain control of the Persian Church and to persecute and expel the orthodox.

After the Persian Christians had fallen into heresy

they grew strong in numbers and spread their beliefs throughout a great part of Asia. At one time their pseudo-Church spread so far to the East and counted so many bishops that it seemed a rival to Christ's Church itself in extent, power and missionary zeal.

Even the advent of Mahommedanism did not at first crush this vigorous sect, and for some time it was doubtful if Central Asia would become Christian or Moslem.

At length, however, Mahommedanism conquered and Christianity disappeared gradually before it, so that to-day all that remains of this once so flourishing organisation is a scanty remnant in Asia, on the confines of Persia, isolated and ignorant.

No trace or taint of Nestorianism has ever reappeared among Catholics, but Protestants, if asked to declare their belief in the Incarnation, nearly always define it in terms which prove their underlying Nestorianism. Even when they are willing to say that Jesus Christ is God, they shrink from the Catholic statement, that God was born of Mary; that God shed His blood for us on Calvary; that God died. To-day as in the fifth century, in London as at Ephesus, the honour of Mary is the safeguard, the outpost of the Adoration of Her Son. To acknowledge the Theotokos is to believe in God the Son made man.

X. EUTYCHIANISM

EVERY heresy is an exaggeration or distortion of a truth: and the greater or more important the truth thus untruly held, the greater and worse the heresy. Thus the first truth of Revealed as of Natural Religion is the Divine Unity; yet every Trinitarian heresy from Sabellianism to extreme Arianism came from considering this Fundamental doctrine out of relation to other revealed truths.

So also whenever a great heresy has to be met and conquered there is a danger lest those who, to conquer it, have had to stress the doctrine it attacked, should in time contemplate that doctrine so fixedly and exclusively that other doctrines, necessary to the perfect balance and proportion of the faith, should be lost sight of, belittled or denied.

This is exemplified particularly in the history of the heresy we must next consider. Nestorius and his followers had divided Christ by denying the Unity of His Person. Those who most ardently upheld that Unity of Person fell, or at least some of them fell, into the heresy of denying the existence in Him of two natures.

One of these, Eutyches, was Archimandrite of a Constantinopolitan monastery, and had been a valiant defender of the true faith against Nestorius and all Nestorians.

By the year 448 he had unfortunately got, as we should say to-day, Nestorianism on the brain—and saw evidences of concealed Nestorianism everywhere. Among those whom he accused of this heresy was Eusebius, Bishop of Dorylaeum—an accusation which could only have been brought by a disordered mind, since some eighteen years before Eusebius had honourably distinguished himself by detecting and denouncing the

heresy of Nestorius at its beginning. Righteously indig-
nant that he should now be accused of a heresy he had
always abhorred, he brought before a synod at Constantinople a counter-charge of heresy against his accuser.

Eutyches was therefore ordered to present himself and
confront Eusebius before the synod. At first he refused
to attend, and only after many delays and protests
did he do so. He was there questioned as to whether
he admitted that in Christ there were two Natures after
the Union, and that Christ was consubstantial according
to the flesh with us. After some controversy he accepted
the latter doctrine, but refused to profess Christ's existence in two Natures. "*Of* two Natures—but not *In*
two Natures," he said.

Eutyches was therefore deposed and excommunicated.
He appealed from the synod to the Pope, Leo I, and
to the Emperor and the Bishop of Constantinople.
Flavian also wrote to the Pope declaring the heresies
Eutyches had owned before the synod.

The Emperor called together a Council to be held
again at Ephesus, and the Pope condemned Eutyches
and sent by his legates his famous Tome or Dogmatic
Letter, defining the true doctrine of the Incarnation to
be read before the Council. When the Council came
together it was composed of the partisans of Eutyches.
Dioscurus, Patriarch of Alexandria, who presided, refused
to acknowledge the authority of the papal envoys or
to read the papal letters. They deposed the orthodox
Bishop of Constantinople and Eusebius of Dorylaeum,
and restored Eutyches to his monastery and dignity.

When St. Leo heard how this Council (to be known
in future ages as the Robber Council on account of the
violence displayed therein) had acted, he condemned
it and annulled its decrees in a local Roman synod and
requested the Emperor to call a fresh Council.

This the Emperor, under the influence of Dioscurus and Eutyches, utterly refused to do, but after the Emperor's death in 450, the new Emperor, Marcian, expressed his willingness to comply with the Pope's wish. At length, in October 451, the Council began its deliberations at Chalcedon, near Constantinople.

It was a Council consisting mainly of Eastern bishops, yet it accepted as president the Pope's legate, and when St. Leo's famous letter was read they acclaimed it, shouting, "Peter has spoken by Leo."

At this Council Eutyches and Dioscurus were deposed and excommunicated, and, more important, the doctrine of the two distinct natures existing in the one person of Jesus Christ was explicitly defined.

As the Council of Ephesus was followed by a great schism, so also was the Council of Chalcedon. But whilst the Nestorian sect has dwindled to a miserable remnant, large bodies of Christians in Egypt and throughout the Near East have remained in heresy and schism ever since their bishops broke away from Catholic Unity rather than accept the definitions of Chalcedon.

To many it has seemed that Eutyches and his fellows were hardly dealt with. After all, they say, their error arose from their very anxiety to safeguard the honour of Jesus Christ. It was their horror of the heresy that would divide Him that led them by over-emphasis to fall into the opposite error.

Yet while this heresy is at first view less shocking to the adorer of Our Lord than that which denies in effect His true Godhead, yet in reality it is no less destructive of the Incarnation.

"*Of* two Natures" or "*in* two Natures," seems a difference far too little for which to drive thousands out of the Church, or to be an occasion of a schism so wide and so longlived. A further study of the result of rejecting the true definition may help us to see how great was the peril from which Chalcedon saved the Faith. "One nature only after the Union," they cried. Christ's flesh, they said, was not of the same nature as ours—some went on to say that it was by nature incorruptible and impassible.

But just as the value of Christ's atonement rests on the Unity of His Person, so that to deny that God was born and died is to leave the Passion a merely human suffering, insufficient to atone for the sin of the world—so to deny the reality of Christ's human nature is to make the Passion in any real sense impossible, and to make the example of Christ's human life valueless to us.

If in assuming our human nature the Word had so changed it, so absorbed it, into the divinity that we could no longer say that He was of our very nature, consubstantial with us, then He would no longer be in truth the New Adam, neither could He have suffered, nor could St. Paul have declared Him to be our High Priest, tempted in all points as we are, yet without sin.

If the Divine and the human Natures did not remain in Christ as eternally distinct as they are uniquely united, then either the two natures would be so mixed that Christ would be neither True God nor true Man, but some impossible being compounded of both—or else the Godhead would have so absorbed the Manhood that for all that matters the Incarnation would be but a phrase.

In either case Jesus Christ would no longer be the New Adam—our Elder Brother or Our Example. We could no longer go to Him with our sorrows or trials as to one who knew by *experience* human suffering and human weakness.

D

So by the decrees of these two great Councils of Ephesus and Chalcedon the main outlines of the great dogma of the Incarnation were traced for all time. Henceforward the Church had but to brood prayerfully over this great Mystery, whilst theologians deduced consequence after consequence and saints and mystics could realise in themselves and show forth to others aspect after aspect—detail after detail. So that every generation knows Christ not less but more clearly, more vividly, than the generation before it, the faithful ever increasing their grasp of the Truth, the riches of which all generations to the end of time cannot suffice to exhaust.

XI. MONOTHELITISM

FROM the ashes of the Monophysite heresy, however, there arises another error which is famous to-day not so much for itself as for the scandal it brought upon the Holy See.

The condemnation of Honorius as the favourer of heresy is well known to many who would be in great difficulty if asked what heresy he favoured or what truth he endangered.

The Egyptians had taken up the Monophysite heresy largely as a national cry. Alexandria and Antioch stood always as rivals, and the fact that the school of Antioch held views which, pushed to their logical conclusion, resulted in Nestorianism, was enough to make the Egyptians hold the doctrine opposed to it in so violent and exaggerated a way that they went to the other extreme and fell, as we saw, into Monophysitism.

After the Council of Chalcedon the Emperor backed its decrees with all the power of the State. The Egyptians, who saw in this an insult to their leaders and an outrage on their patriotism, became only the more embittered against the Council and its adherents.

Moreover, they considered, not without reason, that they had been unfairly treated and misrepresented, for though their denial of the existence of two Natures in Christ after the Incarnation really entailed all the consequences detailed above, yet the more responsible leaders violently disclaimed them.

At this juncture the Emperor Heraclius, Sergius, Patriarch of Constantinople, and Cyrus, Patriarch of Alexandria, made a well-meant but ill-judged attempt to pacify the Egyptians and lead them back to the Unity of Faith.

The matter is first mooted in the year 634 in a letter from the Patriarch of Constantinople to the Pope, Honorius, in which Sergius propounds a difficulty.

Cyrus, Patriarch of Alexandria, had brought many of the Monophysites of his diocese to submit to the Church and to sign a formula which affirmed Christ to be "in two natures." So far so good; but alas! it went on to affirm that He worked His divine and human works by "one theandric operation." The complacency of Cyrus, however, was short-lived. Sophronius, a holy and clear-sighted Palestinian monk, did not share in the rejoicing. From Cyrus to Sergius he went, and protested against the one operation most vigorously, and, as we shall see later, most justly: for the expression contained the very quintessence of the old already condemned Monophysitism. Wrought on by the insistence of Sophronius, Sergius had written to Cyrus that it would be well to drop the expression, but that it would also be well not to affirm the contrary. Therefore, he writes to the Pope and submits the case to him.

This was the moment at which the heresy should have been summarily dealt with. Had Honorius been another Leo, the triumph of Chalcedon would have been repeated.

Honorius, however, was of the intellectually lazy type which prefers Peace to Truth; perhaps, also, he wished to avoid disturbing the Emperor's satisfaction at the hardly effected Union in Egypt. At all events, instead of boldly defining the truth, he forbade indeed the heretical formula but equally forbade the enunciation of the truth.

Emboldened by this Sergius drew up in 638 an exposition of doctrine which the Emperor authorised and enforced.

In this exposition, which became known as the *Ecthesis of Heraclius*, the affirmation of one operation or of two operations was equally forbidden. Moreover, it goes on to declare that in Christ there is but one will.

Honorius had meanwhile died, but Pope Severinus, when the *Ecthesis* was brought before him, immediately condemned it.

It was not until October 649 that the solemn ex-cathedra definition, which Honorius should have made, was at last pronounced. The Pope, St. Martin, presiding over a Council at the Lateran, condemned Sergius, Cyrus, and other Monothelite leaders by name, together with the *Ecthesis* and a later document of the same trend known as the *Type of Constans*.

St. Martin atoned for the laziness or indecision of Honorius by giving his life in witness to the Faith he had defined.

A Monothelite Emperor, Constans, now reigned. He had the Pope kidnapped and carried to Constantinople, whence, as he steadfastly refused to accept the *Ecthesis*, he was exiled to the Crimea, where he died a martyr's death.

Monothelitism was finally crushed in the Sixth General Council at Constantinople, which condemned not only all the heretics who taught Monothelitism, but also Honorius. Honorius was condemned not for teaching falsely but for not teaching truly. By defining the true doctrine he could have stamped out the heresy which his refusal to face the question allowed to flourish un-checked.

To practical and blunt-minded Westerners it may seem strange that so subtle a question should have excited whole cities to turmoil—or that for the sake of his view of it an Emperor should kidnap a Pope—even if we understand that, once the subject was in dis-pute, a Pope should die rather than accept or promulgate false doctrine concerning it.

We must, however, remember that while the Greeks and the Eastern theologians generally were more ready to raise metaphysical questions concerning the Trinity and the Incarnation than were their Western fellow-bishops, this question was taken up by many for less intellectual reasons.

Monophysitism, as we saw above, was presented to the Egyptian as the doctrine upheld by his national saints and heroes, especially by St. Cyril.

St. Cyril, in his controversy with Nestorius, had used the easily misunderstood expression, "We confess One Nature of the Word Incarnate." By this St. Cyril meant simply that the Nature of the Word was not in any way altered by the assumption of the humanity. The Monophysites, however, understood him to mean that in the Incarnation the Divine and Human natures became one not only in Person and Hypostasis, but, in some strange sense, "One in Nature." They, therefore, rejected and loathed the Council of Chalcedon because they thought that it undid the work of the Council of Ephesus and lowered the prestige of St. Cyril and of the Egyptian Church.

When the Monophysites agreed as the price of Catholic Communion to accept the orthodox dogma that "Christ exists in two Natures," they still held that the union between those two natures was of such a kind that the human nature was no longer capable of its own distinct natural acts.

Not only, they held, were the human acts of Christ the acts of a Divine Person—"in which they were perfectly orthodox"—but they went on to say they are worked not by a human but by a "theandric" operation. By saying this they deprived the doctrine of the Incarnation of its very core and centre.

In vain do we say that God has assumed human

nature—if we deny to that Nature a human will—since
it is precisely in the free intellectual will that the dignity
of human nature consists. In vain again do we grant
to Humanity a human will unless that human will
has its own proper operation. The obedience of Christ
by which He suffered for us must be the free human act
of a human will submitting itself to the Divine Will—
which is impossible if the human will of Christ has not
an activity or operation of its own—distinct from,
though altogether submissive to, the Divine Will. We
somewhat confuse the question by using the word "Will"
sometimes of the thing chosen, sometimes of the act of
choosing. Thus we say "Your will is mine," meaning
"the choice of my will agrees with yours."

In this sense of course we may say the Divine and
human will in Christ were one, but in its proper sense,
of the faculty and the act of the faculty, that is to say—
the power by which we choose and the act of choosing,
Christ's will as Man was altogether distinct from and
submissive to His will as God.

As we said at the conclusion of the last section, Ephesus
and Chalcedon settled once for all this and all other
questions concerning the Incarnation.

Christ is perfect God and perfect Man United in One
Person. This Monothelite controversy was settled before
it was raised, in the decision that the Two perfect Natures
existed—without confusion—in the Unity of One Person.

XII. PELAGIANISM

ABSORBED by the deep problems involved in that supreme mystery of the Incarnation, the Church in the first four centuries had not developed, in detail, the doctrines concerning man's ruin and renewal. She taught, indeed, everywhere that man was free, and also, that by the fall he was ruined and had lost his right to heaven, which he could regain only by the merit of Christ Crucified. The spirit of the East was, as it is now, fatalistic, and against this, theologians of the Eastern Church stressed the doctrine of man's freedom and responsibility, while in the West, less liable to this error, it was safe to stress equally the converse truth of man's utter inability to do anything whatsoever towards salvation without the grace of God.

It was, however, in the West that that self-sufficient heresy arose which, by rejecting the truth of the necessity of Grace in the name of man's freewill, forced theologians to study all the implications of Scripture and Tradition, and occasioned the long series of decrees and definitions on Grace and Freewill beginning from the Council of Carthage in May 418, and not yet complete—since many questions, raised and warmly debated during the last three centuries, await definition.

There lived in Rome during the first decade of the fifth century a monk from the British Isles named Pelagius. Though not in holy orders, he wrote theological treatises in which he inculcated the heresy which bears his name. From Rome, together with his friend Caelestius, he passed to North Africa, where Caelestius sought ordination, but was refused, as he had imbibed and taught more openly than Pelagius the latter's heresy.

Detected in Africa, Caelestius journeyed into Asia

Minor, and was ordained in Ephesus, leaving his heresy spreading like mildew in Carthage.

St. Augustine rose to defend the Faith with his powerful pen, and began the great treatises which have gained for him the title "Doctor of Grace."

While Augustine strove to cleanse Africa from the corruption, Pelagius was spreading it in the East.

St. Jerome wrote against him, and he was cited twice before ecclesiastical authorities, but by adroit twisting, and sometimes owing to his opponents' lacking facility in Greek, he evaded condemnation.

At length the matter was referred to the Holy See, and Pope Innocent I excommunicated Pelagius and Caelestius. The Pope, dying shortly afterwards, was succeeded by Pope Zosymus, to whom the two heresiarchs appealed, denying that they held the condemned doctrines.

The Pope, therefore, ordered that they be summoned before a Council and there condemned or re-admitted to communion. A Council was, therefore, held in Carthage, which on the 1st of May, 418, solemnly and finally condemned them and defined the doctrines against which they had erred.

Their principal errors were the following:—

They denied original sin, and that death and concupiscence resulted from Adam's fall.

They taught that man was able, by the ordinary powers given to his nature, to avoid sin and reach heaven.

Forgiveness of sin through faith means forgiveness from punishment, not renewal in grace.

The Law is equal to the Gospel as a guide to heaven.

Men can by training their wills live without sin, and have done so, not only since Christ, but also before.

Against these heresies the Council of Carthage laid down:—

1. That death, in Adam, was the result of sin.
2. That new-born children needed baptism on account of original sin.
3. That grace is not only needed for knowledge of God's commandments, but also for strength to obey them.
4. That without grace it is impossible to perform good works.

The State enforced the decrees of the Church. Pelagians were banished by an Imperial rescript from Italy. The Semi-Pelagians taught that though men could not merit salvation yet by natural good works they could in some sense deserve grace.

And once in a state of salvation they held that man could attain final perseverance without any special gratuitous grace from God.

Some at least, also, met the crucial difficulty of reconciling God's will that all should be saved, with the death of unbaptised infants, with the astonishing solution that it was on account of their foreseen want of faith had they lived!

The controversy was prolonged and the tide of opinion veered now to one extreme, now to the other, but finally, at the Ecumenical Council of Orange, these opinions, since known as Semi-Pelagianism, were condemned as heresy, and a solemn definition given of man's utter inability to do anything whatever by his own natural powers towards salvation, and of the absolute necessity of grace before man can move at all towards faith or salvation.

As we saw above, much was still left for the Church

to decide in future ages. Orthodox theologians, in their anxiety to make clear man's inability to do works fit for heaven, did not always distinguish between such supernatural works and works good in the natural order.

In denying the contention of Pelagius, that Adam's death was not a punishment for sin but due to his corporeal nature, they did not say precisely why Adam was not originally destined for death, nor do they make clear the exact relation between concupiscence and sin. But it is to St. Augustine and his fellow-labourers, to the Councils and the Popes who condemned Pelagianism and Semi-Pelagianism, that we owe our knowledge of the wonders of God's love—the dignity of the soul which God invites, illumines, crowns, by His Redeeming and Sanctifying Grace.

XIII. CATHARISM

ABOUT the eleventh century a heresy, as variable as it was poisonous, appeared sporadically in many parts of Europe. We have called it a heresy, but the teaching and system of the "Cathari" or "pure ones" was not that distortion of some part of Christian teaching to the denial of other Christian doctrines, which is heresy, but an altogether alien and contradictory religion into which some few Christian terms had been forced and, in being so forced, had also been twisted into travesties of themselves.

Manicheeism, which had during the fifth century provoked to battle with it the greatest minds of Christendom, was by the zeal of the bishops, backed by rigorous enactments of the emperors, extirpated from Europe and driven to the East and to Africa, in which last mentioned territory it waged its final struggle with the Western Church.

Some four hundred years later, in the early years of the eleventh century, a teaching strangely similar to this long past error once more appeared among Christian peoples. For nearly four hundred years it was a constant peril to the purity of the Faith. Nor was the danger to the Church only, but to all civil government, and, indeed, to human society as a whole. This teaching attacked not only revealed religion, but those first principles of Natural Religion and Ethics on which human knowledge and rational human conduct are alike based; and which are at the basis of those institutions by which man forms a society and not a mere herd.

England, safeguarded equally by her insular position and by the proverbial slowness of the English mind to accept new ideas, true or false, suffered less than other parts of Europe. Yet even here, a band of German-speaking Cathari who had fled from the Continent were, after due ecclesiastical condemnation, sentenced by Henry II in 1166 to branding and exposure, from which they died.

Catharism had within itself many sects and divisions —all, however, agreed in teaching that God is not the creator of this material world, which, on the contrary, was created by an evil principle. This principle, as some sects taught, was a rebellious creature of the first Principle; others held that it was a co-existent Principle, the source of all evil, as the First is of all good.

Since it is impossible to describe all the varieties of error held by each one of the Catharistic sects we shall attend chiefly to that sect which is, to us, better known than the rest. First, on account of its connection with Simon de Montfort; secondly, because it was the occasion of the institution of the Inquisition.

The Albigenses appeared in Italy and southern France in the twelfth century, and not content with preaching subversive tenets, proceeded to enforce their teaching by carnage and spoliation, so that the second Council of the Lateran, in 1179, called on Christians to rise in defence of their Christian heritage, and in aid of the country about Albi and Toulouse, which the Albigenses were devastating. Their teaching was as follows: first they taught the dualistic theory set forth above—then that man was a combination of two opposing and irreconcilable principles, a spiritual being created by the Good God having been deceived by the evil principle and thrust into a material body of which he, the evil one, was the creator. The whole aim of Albigensianism was to deliver this creature of God, the soul, from its hateful imprisonment in matter. The imprisonment they taught was made more strait and oppressive by every concession to the demands of the body.

So they taught that procreation was of all evils the worst, since it not only defiled the soul of the parents by sexual indulgence but entailed the possible consequence of imprisoning in vile flesh yet another spiritual creature.

Whilst strict continence was desirable Christian marriage was worse than any vicious excess, since it not only involved a permanent state of incontinence but was entered into for the very purpose of begetting offspring.

Those members of the sect who had received the "*consolamentum*," and had been thereby admitted to the number of the perfect—who alone could obtain immediate salvation after this life—were bound to perpetual continence, to long fasts and abstinence from many kinds of food. These kinds of food, as well as marital intercourse, were allowed to those catechumens who had only promised to receive the *consolamentum* before death.

With a prudence approaching cynicism, the ministers of this sect mistrusted the perseverance, in so rigid a rule of life, of those who delayed incurring the obligation till they found themselves about to renounce all fleshly delights willy-nilly at the call of death. If such an initiate should, contrary to all expectation, show signs of recovery it was thought well to safeguard him from a spiritual relapse by persuading him to undertake the *endura*—a fast prolonged to starvation—and should the patient be faint-hearted enough to break down and call for food, his friends were urged in his highest interests to withhold it.

Since matter was essentially evil, an Incarnation of God was impossible. Jesus had no real body and only feigned to be born of Mary. Thus He had no true manhood nor on the other hand was He true God, but only one of the highest of pure Spirits appearing on earth to deliver man by His example and teaching from the delusions of the flesh. As they taught that salvation is the deliverance of man's soul from its fleshly prison, there is no Resurrection.

Such were the tenets of the fanatics who at the time of the second Council of the Lateran were endeavouring by force of arms to uproot Christianity in southern France.

Fifteen years later the danger had become more pressing. The new Count of Toulouse, Raymond VI, was definitely favouring the heresy, and under his protection the poison was spreading far and wide.

Frightened by the effect on neighbouring princes of the Pope's call to arms, he submitted in 1208, promising himself to drive all heretics from his domains. Now also aid was at hand from an army more dangerous to heresy than any that secular princes could send to the field. No error, however fundamental, can live except by the presence under it, or mixed with it, of some distorted truth. The secret of the influence of the Albigenses and other Catharists lay in the self-denial and mortification of the preachers.

The mob then, as now, were slow to reason—slow to detect blasphemy under seemingly pious talk—but all could contrast the poor dress and meagre diet of the new teachers with the wealth and, too often, the ostentation of the orthodox clergy. All could see the point of the contrast drawn between the labouring Apostle and the luxurious Abbot or Bishop.

Armies might compel submission, but no brute force could compel men to renounce their admiration for unworldliness and self-denial. At this juncture appears one of the greatest figures in the Church's history. In the train of Diego, Bishop of Osma, there came to the papal legate, Dominic Guzman, to be known to countless generations as St. Dominic, the founder of the preaching friars.

A strange exchange has taken place in modern minds between St. Dominic and his great contemporary, St. Francis of Assisi. St. Francis has been thought the friend of humanity, St. Dominic, the stark ascetic, loving God but neglecting humanity. Yet St. Francis' poverty, praised by so many lovers of humanity, was embraced by him purely for the sake of the Crucified, whilst St. Dominic adopted the same poverty as an heroic exercise of fraternal charity.

The heretics were subverting souls by a wrong preaching of asceticism. Dominic will meet them on their own ground, and by true Christian asceticism will win men's hearts, so that their minds may be opened to God's truth. He was not, however, given time to bring back the heretics by prayer and preaching.

Innocent III, alarmed by the ever-widening spread of the heresy, called on the King of France to take action against Raymond and his supporters.

Nobles flocked to join the crusade against heresy, moved equally by a hatred of heresy and love of the heretics' possessions—these latter being forfeit, and to be gained by gallant and grasping Christians. Raymond, terrified, submitted once more and himself joined the crusade, which was led now by the English Simon de Montfort.

Soon the crusade became simply a war of invasion and a means of land-grabbing. Atrocities on the part of Albigenses were met with atrocious reprisals by the Catholics, and eventually all Raymond's possessions were ceded to the crown of France, and, man's fury having worked itself out in blood, God's truth was left to overcome, as it could, the original evil, made all the more bitter by many a hate and blood feud.

To this task the sons of St. Dominic set themselves, by prayer, by preaching, and by stern judgment. To them was entrusted the office of Inquisitors, to whom it belonged to sift all cases of suspected heresy, to save those whom ignorant zeal or jealous malice accused unjustly, to teach and reclaim those who had been led astray, and in case of obstinacy to declare the offender an enemy of the Christian name, one whom the Church, unable truthfully to claim, left to the vengeance of the Christian State against whose fundamental laws he rebelled.

The long and arduous task was at length successful, and by the end of the fourteenth century Albigensianism, with all other forms of Catharism, was practically extinct.

Modern civilisation has as scant mercy for Inquisitors as they had for heresy, and a good deal of sentimental admiration and pity has been expended on mediæval heretics, yet to the defenders of the Faith modern Europe owes far more than it dreams. Imagine a world in which Albigensianism prevailed.

All society is built on the family—all progress on the instinctive knowledge of the dignity of human nature— the worth alike of human instincts and human judgments. This anti-human heresy, by destroying the sanctity of the family, would reduce mankind to a horde of unclean beasts: by denying the essential goodness of human nature, as such, would make progress and stability alike impossible—the only rational act of mankind a universal suicide.

E

XIV. THE WALDENSIANS

As has been said, heresies arise from a truth held out of due proportion, insisted upon to the ignoring or denial of other truths.

More strangely still, during the Middle Ages, an excessive insistence on the Evangelical counsel of poverty, to the detriment of other virtues, was the occasion and beginning of many heresies.

As Europe gradually became Christian, converted chiefs and kings poured out upon the Church and her ministers riches of land and of goods. Some of these, fired with devotion, desired, like the Magi, to offer to Christ gifts of all they held most precious. Others again repenting of past crimes, built monasteries and richly endowed them in order to share in the merits of the lives of penance and reparation lived therein.

As Europe recovered from the upheaval and confusion which followed the break-up of the Roman power, the feudal system was gradually established; the bishops and abbots becoming feudal lords.

It was inevitable that such positions should be coveted by greedy and ambitious men; that princes should seek to secure them for partisans, who, in return, should uphold their patron's cause—even to the detriment of ecclesiastical discipline—or should intrude into them their own needy or grasping kinsfolk.

It was the scandal caused by so much worldliness in the Church which led in the twelfth and thirteenth centuries to a great esteem for Evangelical Poverty. Some of the outcry against priest and prelate doubtless arose from envy, but yet many of the murmurs arose from honest hearts anxious for the victory of good over evil.

Many, seeing the harm to the Church that riches had

brought about, thought that if only she would cast them from her the holiness of the first age would return.

The whole world to-day loves and marvels at the Poor Man of Assisi. No other Catholic Saint, probably no other mediæval character, is so widely known, so loved by many and varied men.

The supreme irony of this is, that outside the Catholic Church speakers and writers continually claim St. Francis as the great Individualist—one who cared nothing for authority and very little for dogma, a forerunner of the sentimental pietist of to-day. Whereas, in fact, the whole secret of his success and of the vitality of his influence was his reverential love of Church and Priesthood, his realisation of the oneness of Christ and the Church.

Francis, reading in the Gospel Christ's directions to His first lay preachers, accepted them as led to himself personally, and stripped himself not only of wealth or even conveniences, but of the most ordinary necessaries of life, to follow in utter poverty—the Poor Christ. He was not the first in the mediæval Church to hear and accept that call.

Among others who heard it, Waldo, the merchant of Lyons, holds a melancholy pre-eminence.

Like Francis, he became influenced with love of the poverty of Jesus: like Francis, he sought in the Gospel the rule by which to imitate that poverty: but, unlike Francis, while imitating the poverty, he ignored the humility and obedience of his Divine Model, and so the path of poverty which led Francis to the heights of seraphic virtue led Waldo to the horrible eminence of heresiarch. Whilst Francis was the great Rebuilder the times needed, Waldo's name stands only among those who destroy.

On the Feast of the Assumption, 1176, Waldo cast away the last of his worldly possessions. His example was imitated and soon a large number of his followers, renouncing all they possessed, roamed the country, speaking to all they met about the things of God.

So far we seem to see an anticipation of the Franciscan movement, but now appears the fatal flaw. St. Francis who, from his deep reverence, refused to receive the burden of the priesthood, held the teaching Church in far too much honour to advance speculation opposed to her teaching.   He and his followers presupposed in all their popular exhortations the dogmas of the Faith. It was the practical consequences of those dogmas they urged on their hearers, the dogmas themselves were unquestioned. The Love of God, compassion for Jesus crucified, the love of the Divine Babe of Bethlehem, the dignity of all things pertaining to our Lord's Sacramental life, these were the subjects of their meditations, these the objects which, displayed before men's minds, brought whole multitudes to contrition, led many to the way of Perfection.

The followers of Waldo lacked both the love and the humility of the Franciscans. Despite their lack of theological training they boldly attempted not only to speculate but to criticise and even to preach against revealed doctrine.

So soon did their heretical tendency appear that, in less than ten years from their first appearance, they had been banned by Bishop, Council and Pope.

Beginning with an exaggerated doctrine on Evangelical poverty, they went on to deny the power of keys to the Catholic priesthood, to deny purgatory and indulgences. They anticipated modern Protestants in their comprehensiveness and willingness to receive new heresies from any quarter. An extreme pacifism seems to point to Catharistic influence, while, as they lingered on with varying fortunes through the century, they fraternised in turn with each new heresy that appeared.

When Protestantism arose the Waldenses of the various countries infected made common cause with the new heretics and cheerfully adopted the dogmas or rather denials of their new associates. Finally they for the most part coalesced with the various Protestant bodies. Those scattered fragments which survive independently differ in name only from the other Protestant sects.

XV. PROTESTANTISM

MOST people if asked to-day what was the prime error of Protestantism would hesitate how to reply. Perhaps they would settle on its rejection of the Sacramental theory, or on its claim to the right of private interpretation of the Scriptures: but while to-day its exponents and opponents alike would fix upon these as the main points in dispute, the heresy originated in a denial more fundamental still—the denial of the Catholic doctrine of Grace.

According to Catholic teaching man at his creation was dowered by God not only with all those attributes proper to his nature as a rational animal—the link between the merely sensitive and the purely intellectual creation—but also with other qualities and powers immeasurably above these, which raised him from the natural state of a rational creature—the state of God's servant— to the supernatural state of an adopted Son of God. These gifts, however, depended for their continuance on the fidelity of Adam in the service of his Creator.

Adam sinned and thereby not only incurred the punishment of a disobedient servant, but also the forfeiture of his adopted sonship.

The punishment of Adam's personal sin fell on him alone—but the forfeiture affected also his descendants— since God had willed to raise to adopted sonship not simply Adam's person but Adam's race. The human race fell in Adam—but fell, not from a natural to an unnatural state—but rather from a supernatural to a merely natural one. Man still retained what was proper to his nature— the essential powers of Intellect and Will—though now his Intellect was darkened, and his Will enfeebled, not precisely by the Fall itself but by the consequence of the Fall.

Moreover, the conflict necessarily resulting from man's compound nature was left to work out its consequences —without that special regulating and controlling gift which God had vouchsafed to his son Adam in his innocence.

Man could, however, still do works good in themselves —he could still practise, at least sometimes, natural virtues, and these acts being good were pleasing to God— since it is always pleasing to God that the creature should act in accordance with the nature He has given it. Such acts, however, being merely natural, could have no relation to the supernatural order—nor could they directly or indirectly avail for Heaven—which is the supernatural possession of God by Beatific Vision.

Moreover, God, for the sake of Jesus Christ, invites men to receive once more the grace of adoption and the forgiveness of sins, and enables him to accept it, man being able freely to accept or freely reject this invitation.

Such is a brief and necessarily inadequate statement of the doctrine—which the heresiarch Luther so attacked and distorted that to-day, outside the Church, it is not enough to say that the doctrine is denied; the very knowledge of it no longer exists.

Luther was an Augustinian Friar who had entered Religion in consequence of a vow taken in a moment of extreme emotional disturbance. At first his life seems to have been a regular and zealous one, but after some years —on being entrusted with the onerous duties of Lecturer in Sacred Scripture—and burdened with much other exterior business—his own spiritual life began to suffer. His most binding monastic duties were left unperformed— and periods of undisciplined neglect alternated with periods of equally undisciplined penance. In vain did his superiors point out to him the dangers of his way of life. He utterly refused to tread the slow plodding path to self-conquest and peace, and would follow only his own self-chosen way. At length, worn out with his violent recoils from one extreme to another, he imagined he saw a short cut out of all his difficulties. Struck by the insistence of St. Paul on the necessity of Faith for salvation, he ignored the equal insistence on Love and Repentance in other passages, and decided to cease all his efforts at penance and amendment, trusting for his salvation—to his confidence in Christ's Redemption alone.

Such was the new gospel which Luther set out to teach. At first he taught it without renouncing other Catholic dogmas; but little by little, as the full bearing of the heresy was realised, the whole doctrine of Grace—Fall—Redemption—Sacraments was seen to be involved.

Luther had found his passions hard to combat—his will weak against temptation. Now he taught that the Fall had so completely ruined man's nature that it was hopelessly corrupt, the helpless slave of passion, and that man's will was so far from being free that he was equally unable to reject the inspirations of God or the temptations of the devil. Man's nature being thus corrupt, nothing is left for Grace to seize upon and elevate.

Therefore, according to Luther, Grace is not a physical reality created by God in the soul and making it holy, but simply God's good will towards the soul, by which He regards and treats it, though unholy, as though it were holy; for the sake of Christ's holiness. In one sentence—

The Church teaches that God for Christ's sake *imparts* holiness:

Luther taught that God for Christ's sake *imputes* holiness to the sinner.

It would be untrue and unfair to picture the world of Luther's day as a world of peace and faith, the tranquillity of which was shattered by the publication of Luther's heresy.

Vast scandal was caused by the lives of Popes and prelates—notoriously impure of life as was Alexander; far more zealous for Art and Literature than for the Faith as Leo; or again, like Julius, Italian prince rather than Universal Pope, and caring before all for the defence of the Temporal Sovereignty. To this scandal was added all the unrest caused by the growing spirit of Nationality and the perennial stress and conflict between Teutonic and Latin ideals and temperaments. The whole Empire, Roman in name, Germanic in fact, was a huge mass of fuel, soaked in various highly inflammable spirits, into which the publication of Luther's famous Ninety-five Theses cast the fatal spark.

The immediate occasion of their publication was as follows: Leo X had granted an Indulgence to all who contributed to the fund for rebuilding the great church and shrine of St. Peter's. Now this was in itself quite unexceptionable. Indulgences during the Middle Ages were constantly granted for such acts of charity—as the building of churches, the repairing of bridges, going on, or helping to equip, Crusades: and the rebuilding of the great church at Rome in which lay buried the Prince of the Apostles, together with the Apostles of the Gentiles, was an Act of Faith and Love in which the whole Christian World might well be asked to join.

The cause of offence lay in the manner in which the alms of the faithful were collected. The indulgence was offered and the money was to be conveyed to the Holy See *via* Albert, Bishop of Brandenburg, who was to have in return some part of the moneys collected. The actual preaching of the Indulgence was in the hands of Tetzel, a Dominican friar—who, though by no means the monster of blasphemy and mendacity that he appears in the writings of his opponents, yet seems to have been more zealous for the success of his appeal to the generosity of his hearers than careful to protect them from the possibility of mistake or exaggeration regarding the power of Indulgences.

The publication of the Indulgence roused Luther to fury, on motives good, indifferent, and bad. The real possibilities of abuse, the German dislike of German money going to enrich and embellish Rome, the way in which the doctrine of Indulgences sums up, implies and includes the true doctrine on Sin, Grace, Freewill, Repentance, Communion of Saints, Jurisdiction of the Pope—all these reasons drove Luther to embody his opposition in ninety-five theses which, according to the custom of the time, he nailed up on the door of the castle church at Wittenberg on October 31st, 1517, as a challenge to disputation.

The storm had broken indeed. The humanistic Pope who, with the contempt for Monasticism and Scholasticism then fashionable in cultured circles, had till then treated the matter as a mere dispute between Augustinian and Dominican, awoke at length to the danger.

By the Bull *Exsurge Domine*, Luther's doctrines were authoritatively condemned, and he himself ordered to recant within sixty days under pain of excommunication. The Bull was issued in July, 1520, but Luther openly defied it, and on its arrival in Wittenberg, burned it amidst the jeers and scoffings of the University students.

Summoned before the Diet, Luther refused to submit; but before the safe conduct, which the Emperor had granted him to attend it, could expire and the ban of the Empire which he had incurred could involve him in its consequences, he was spirited away by friends to a fortress where he was safe from the Law. Here in the Wartburg he remained until the revolt from Rome had so far progressed that at Wittenberg the religion practised could no longer be called in any sense Catholic.

Luther had claimed for every man the right to judge what was the sense of Scripture, independently of the Church, but was naïvely surprised when he found any man judging the same independently of Luther. But men had not rejected an infallible Church to accept an infallible ex-friar. Soon the whole of Germany and Switzerland was a welter of quarrelling sects.

Luther denied the Mass, but accepted the Real Presence. Calvin, later, and Zwingli denied both, though Calvin admitted a virtual presence which Zwingli denied. A hundred lesser leaders appeared, each with his new theory, and against them each and all, as against the Church he had left, Luther wrote and preached with ceaseless energy and vituperation. The main heresies of Luther were accepted, logically worked out and elaborated by Calvin, a French lawyer who, born in France in 1509, accepted the new doctrines in boyhood and gradually, as he advanced in years, gave up the Law, and busied himself with preaching and disputing both with tongue and pen. From time to time he appeared in France and the Netherlands, wherever Protestants were numerous and whenever events favoured the promulgation of the new religion. At length he was invited to Geneva, where the majority of the citizens became Protestants, and at last set up a Church State rather than a State Church, of which Calvin became oracle and lawgiver. His particular contribution to Protestantism was the drawing out in logical sequence of all the principles contained in the new doctrines—on Freewill, Sin, Grace and Salvation.

He denied God's will to save all mankind, taught that God created some to be saved—to the glory of His mercy—others to be eternally lost—to the glory of His justice or rather of His vengeance; for Calvin denied the freedom of man's will and held that men were damned for sins which they were utterly unable to avoid committing. Like Luther, he taught that Faith, in the new sense of a man's confidence in his own election to eternal life, was the only means of salvation. Moreover, this Faith was caused in a sinner's soul by God alone without any co-operation on his own part, the sinner being entirely passive.

These theories, when consistently held, uprooted alike sacraments, morals and even intercessory prayer. What communion in good works could there be, when even the good works of the justified were sins, only unpunishable because worked by one whom God elected for salvation?

To add to the evils of the time, the Council which the prevailing heresies urgently needed was delayed, partly by the jealousy of States, partly, alas, by the sloth of worldly prelates unwilling that ecclesiastical corruptions should be too suddenly reformed. At length, however, after the rejection of one meeting place after another, a General Council met at Trent in 1545.

So many were the questions to be decided, so manifold the abuse to be reformed, that no less than eighteen years elapsed between the opening of the Council and the termination of its labours.

The Faith was clearly defined on all those points which heretics denied.

XVI. ANGLICANISM

THE Church of England, although she has taught or tolerated, severally or together, nearly every shade of Protestant heresy, yet demands separate treatment.

Her supreme distinction among the sects is this: that while Erastianism was, in the case of other denominations, an inevitable and sometimes hated condition—it is the very root and essence of her being.

The struggle between Church and State, Pope and King, was no new thing. From the day when Caesarism found itself utterly vanquished in the attempt to crush the Church from without, it has been engaged in a ceaseless effort to seize and rule it from within—an effort ever failing yet ever renewed. Again and again we see emperors and kings trying to impose their wills upon the Church, claiming a right to appoint bishops, interfering in Papal elections, hindering the publication of Bulls, or the due course of Canon Law, yet always on the pretence of safeguarding their own secular rights, always professing in words the utmost deference for the spiritual jurisdiction of the Holy See. Not until Henry Tudor arose had any monarch dared to attack the doctrine of the Church's visible Unity—or dared to hack from it a separate body of which the monarch should be both king and Pope.

When the bishops of England accepted Henry as the supreme head of Christ's Church in this land, and signed the oath declaring the Pope to have no more jurisdiction here than any other foreign bishop, they laid the very foundation stone of the new system.

It was no empty title which Henry claimed. He had long been accustomed to theological debate and knew well all that Papal Supremacy implied. He had received from the Pope the title of "Defender of the Faith" in reward for his defence of the Seven Sacraments against Luther, and had, contrary to the usual grudging assent of monarchs, gone to the utmost in acknowledging and defending Papal claims. Now finding that supreme judge resolute in defending at once the claims of the weak, and the sanctity of marriage, against a king's lust and obstinacy, he determined to rend the Church and himself usurp, in regard to his own nation, the full Papal prerogatives.

Henry had married in 1509 Katharine of Aragon, the widow of his brother Arthur. The marriage with Arthur, however, though duly solemnised, had not been consummated, and a dispensation from the impediment incurred had been duly and fully granted by the Pope. After eighteen years of wedlock—and after having formed at least a very warm friendship with one of Katharine's maids of honour, Henry's conscience began to be uneasy lest perhaps there should have been a flaw in the dispensation and thereby his marriage be invalidated. In 1528 he caused the Archbishop of Canterbury, Warham, to call him before an ecclesiastical court wherein the validity of his marriage might be tested. Finding the canonical procedure very dilatory, Henry tried first to get a licence for bigamy, then, finding that impossible, to obtain by any means a decree of nullity from the Pope. Finding every expedient useless, at length Henry took the matter into his own hands. The Archbishop of Canterbury died in August 1531, and Henry seized so good an opportunity. Cranmer, a priest well known to Henry as disloyal to the Pope, was summoned back from the continent and nominated Archbishop; the Papal briefs for the consecration were delayed for some time, but finally were granted; and Cranmer was consecrated, taking the oath of fidelity to the Pope with the explicit intention of immediately violating it. Although the king's marriage was then under trial at Rome, Cranmer presumed to adjudicate upon it, and on May 23rd pronounced it invalid. Five days later he declared the king's secret marriage with Anne Boleyn, contracted in the January preceding, to be lawful and valid—a marriage celebrated no one knows when, where, or before whom—celebrated moreover while no court whatever had annulled his first marriage, and while the Pope was peremptorily ordering him to take back his lawful wife.

On this outrage the Pope promptly intervened, excommunicated Henry and declared the proceedings null. But the king had gone too far to retract. Sooner than submit he plunged the whole country into schism and finally into heresy. Already he had forced on the clergy subscription to a document, in which he was styled Supreme Head of the Church—nor could they succeed in their struggles for inserting such qualifying clauses as should explain it in an orthodox sense. He had also forced through the House of Commons an Act abolishing appeals to Rome, and threatening with *Præmunire* any person bringing Bulls of Excommunication into England. Finally the whole schism was consummated by the passing of an Act of Parliament in November, 1535, declaring the king Supreme Head.

Henceforth, all that religious authority which had appertained to the Pope was exercised by the king. He was supreme not only over persons, the old clerical immunities being abolished, but over questions of faith and discipline. Thomas Cromwell, a layman and some time in Wolsey's suite, was commissioned by authority of the king to make a Visitation of Churches and Religious Houses. The benefices throughout the kingdom were valued by royal "commissions" that the first fruits hitherto paid to the Pope might be fully rendered to the royal exchequer.

Every bishop was compelled to sign a formula renouncing his allegiance to the Holy See and acknowledging the Royal Supremacy over the Church. The one bishop courageous enough to refuse, Fisher of Rochester, was beheaded, as was the former Chancellor Sir Thomas More, with a group of Carthusians, a few other monks and friars. But the rest of the bishops, however, reluctantly complied. One by one they renounced their allegiance to Peter and the Church of Peter, to fall under the servitude of Henry's new Church; and servitude it was indeed.

The clergy in convocation were forbidden to pass any law without the king's assent. Cromwell claimed, as the king's vicar-general, the right to preside at its deliberations and authorised Dr. Petre to act as his deputy.

The king, as head of the Church and, therefore, himself the final judge of orthodoxy, conducted in person a trial for heresy. True, the king happened to be this time "on the side of the angels," the man condemned having denied the real presence of Our Lord in the Blessed Sacrament, as well as other Catholic doctrines; but while condemning this heresy, Henry, even by doing so, proclaimed a heresy more fundamental, namely the heresy that the State was the proper judge of doctrine—the fount of teaching and of jurisdiction. And this heresy has been *the* heresy of the Anglican Church ever since. When, after the brief return to Catholic Unity under Mary, England again fell under Elizabeth, it was into this heresy that she fell.

Henry had wished to keep belief in the Mass, Transubstantiation, the Communion of Saints. Edward VI, or rather his political advisers, denied all three. Elizabeth would have wished some approximation to Catholic worship; but all held most firmly to the one fundamental

Anglican doctrine, that "the Church has no authority distinct from and independent of that of the State."

In Tudor days the State was the king—his will was law. As the supreme authority, nominally still vested in the king, passed in practice, more and more, to the Parliament, Parliament became, and still is, the supreme authority in matters of religion to the Anglican Establishment. Individuals, indeed, have protested against this bondage; the whole High Church section studiously ignore this humiliating fact and profess loyalty and subjection to the laws of "The Church"; but exactly *what* they mean by this no one of them seems able or willing to declare. It is by Authority of Parliament that Public Worship has been controlled and regulated from Elizabeth's day till our own. Even when divines sit in Judgment they do so, not by right of any Apostolic jurisdiction, but as commissioned by the State. Bishops take oath that they hold temporalities and spiritualities alike from the sovereign. Kings, indeed, no longer rule the pulpits, choosing the preacher's subject or at times silencing all preaching, but this is not because they now recognise a Church teaching with Divine Authority, supreme in its own sphere, but because all arbitrary government is now dead, and also because the teaching of the Church of England being simply the reflection of the religious thought of the nation, as that thought becomes more and more disconnected and nebulous, freedom must be left for various teachings to suit all the vagaries of the hearers. Despite the devotion, the learning, the personal holiness of thousands of her ministers past and present, the Church of England to-day is essentially the Erastian body her Elizabethan founders made her.

When Henry forced on the English bishops the Oath of Royal Supremacy, they scarcely realised the full

F

blasphemy it implied. When Elizabeth revived it—
taught by the very practical and enlightening commentary
thereon, furnished by the event of two reigns, they refused
it and were deprived of their sees by Royal Authority.
By the same authority new incumbents were appointed
to the (legally) vacant sees, and these new State prelates
acquiesced fully, nay, eagerly, in their own complete
dependence on the State. To-day we see the Archbishop
of Canterbury, the chief pastor of the whole Anglican
hierarchy, protesting, according to the daily press, the
utmost respect for the supreme authority of Parliament
—not in matters of Foreign Policy or Domestic Law—
but of the Public Worship of the Church of England—
and since *Lex Orandi* is *Lex Credendi*, over the Doctrine
that Worship expresses. That laymen should dictate
definitions of dogma to bishops is sufficiently subversive of all idea of a teaching Church; but that a Parliament composed largely of the unbaptised and the un-
believing—even of Jews, Infidels and acknowledged
Atheists, should claim to adjudicate on questions of
Christian worship—is an enormity which is only exceeded
by that of the official representative of the Anglican
clergy acknowledging their claims: thereby renouncing
the Anglican profession to be part of Christ's teaching
Church.

XVII. JANSENISM

It might have been thought that, after the definitions of the Council of Trent, the doctrines of Grace and the Supernatural were safe, but a further and more subtle attack was to come. The fashionable dislike for the Schoolmen had a certain influence even among Catholics, so that when Jansenius, Bishop of Ypres, set out to write a treatise on St. Augustine, he openly professed therein to go behind the commonly received teaching, and to find in St. Augustine the true doctrine on Grace which, he said, was now ignored or denied in the theological schools. His book was the fruit of many years' work and study, and was only completed just before his death. He left it, therefore, for posthumous publication, professing that he submitted the doctrine contained therein to the judgment of the Holy See.

On its publication in 1640, two years after the author's death, it had a rapid and widespread circulation, both in France and Holland, in spite of its condemnation by the Holy Office and the Pope.

Whilst still a young man, Jansenius had formed an intimate friendship with a fellow-student, who by now, had been appointed Abbot of St. Cyran. This friendship was the means of introducing to the French Church a poison from which neither bishops' charges, State proclamations, nor even Papal Bulls were able entirely to free her, for nearly two hundred years.

St. Cyran passed on the heresy of Jansenius, in which he shared, to the religious community at Port Royal, governed by Mére Angélique Arnauld. This community, renowned, in a time of general laxity, for the fervour and strictness of its inmates, had round it a band of sympathetic *dévots* and *dévotes*, through whom its

83

influence on French thought was penetrating. Foremost among them was the family of Mère Angélique Arnauld, one of whom, Dr. Antoine Arnauld, after the death of St. Cyran, published a book "On frequent Communion."

This book was saturated with the teaching and spirit of the condemned *Augustinus*, and was the more dangerous in that, being professedly on a devotional subject, it was read by many whom a theological treatise would have left untouched.

During the Middle Ages, the Holy Communion was approached by the faithful at such long intervals as to necessitate the well-known commandment of the Church of at least yearly communion. At this time an attempt was being made to combat the general coldness by a more frequent approach to this Sacrament of Love. Under pretence of deciding what preparation was necessary for Communion, Arnauld's book practically prohibited all but the most perfect from approaching the altar.

Much controversy ensued; and at last the discussion brought about the intervention of Innocent X, who in 1653 condemned five propositions taken from the works of Jansenius.

Arnauld, faced with the demand that he should subscribe to this condemnation, countered it by condemning the propositions but denying the fact that they were contained in the *Augustinus;* when later, first the bishops and then the Pope bade him condemn not only the five propositions but the book as containing them, he broached the theory that while the Pope can define a doctrine and condemn a heresy opposing it, he cannot infallibly declare such heresy to be contained in any particular book.

This distinction was adopted by most of the Jansenists, and enabled them to pose as persecuted and misunderstood victims, since they were willing, they said, to accept all the Church taught and to anathematise all she condemned, refusing only to swear a fact about one particular book, which fact was no matter of Divine Revelation, and, therefore, no matter of Faith.

In spite of all efforts of bishop or Pope, the heretics refused either to submit to, or openly leave, the Church. By continual publications and insidious arguments they managed to taint even those whom they could not formally corrupt. By artfully playing on the Galican sentiments of otherwise orthodox divines, and by rousing the king's jealousy of Papal prerogatives, they managed to hinder the course of Papal condemnation, so that, while in Holland, the Jansenist leaders, being excommunicated, went into open schism and stood altar against altar—and, therefore, could be fought openly—in France the heretics claimed to be loyal to the Church, and even when exposed and expelled, retained such influence over their former associates that scarcely any part of the French remained altogether untouched.

Jansenism, like Lutheranism and Calvinism, was a heresy concerning Grace but, whereas with these last two, all the heresies of the sect sprung from their false teaching on Grace, with the Jansenists the heresy on Grace seems to have been a result rather than a cause. The theory from which all their false teaching drew its strength being the theory professed by many Anglicans to-day; that the teaching of the Church is something to be searched for in the records of the past rather than something to be heard and accepted in the living present.

The five propositions from Jansenius, around which the battle raged so violently, were as follows:—

1. Some of God's commandments are impossible to just men who wish and strive to keep them, considering

the powers they actually have: the grace by which these commandments may become possible is also wanting.

2. In the state of fallen nature no one ever resists interior grace.

3. In the state of fallen nature—to merit or to deserve punishment, we need not be free from interior necessity, but only from exterior constraint.

4. The Semi-Pelagians, though admitting the necessity of interior preventing grace for all acts, even the beginning of faith, yet fell into heresy in saying that this grace may be either followed or resisted.

5. To say that Christ died or shed His Blood for all men is Semi-Pelagian.

When Jansenius wrote the *Augustinus* from which the condemned propositions were taken, he openly professed to go back from the received teaching of his own day to the purer doctrine of St. Augustine and the Early Church. Apart from how far he twisted the words or meaning of St. Augustine—reading into them his own opinions—the very attempt showed a heretical spirit.

Since the time of St. Augustine, the whole doctrine had developed and crystallised. Distinctions had been drawn to which St. Augustine's theology had not reached, so that to insist on certain phrases of St. Augustine, minus these distinctions, might be as misleading as to revert to the language of some Ante-Nicene writers, even saints and doctors, on the subject of the Incarnation.

As the Jansenists wished to go back in doctrine to the language of the Early Church, so they wished also to apply the discipline of those early centuries in the wholly dissimilar conditions of the sixteenth and seventeenth.

The evils of the time were many and great, and the Church was drawing from her treasures just the new remedies suited for new disorders. These the Jansenists set aside, or violently repudiated, and demanded instead old remedies suited, indeed, to old evils but now useless or even dangerous.

One great remedy for the evils of the day was found in the teaching and practice of the Society of Jesus, especially raised up by God for this very end. It was against the Jesuits as representing the living system that the Jansenists flung themselves.

Heresy, in the name of God's Justice and Sovereignty, had taught doctrines that belittled or denied His Mercy and man's freedom.

The Jesuits sought by insisting on, and reiterating, man's freedom, and above all God's infinite Mercy, to hearten souls driven to despair or recklessness by exclusive insistence on the mystery of Predestination, or God's permission of Sin.

On the doctrinal side the Jansenistic peril was met by condemnation after condemnation of the five propositions above, then of those who claimed a right to reserve their judgment of the *book*, while condemning the doctrines, then for more than a hundred years of book after book—proposition after proposition, tainted with the condemned heresy, or implying in any way that God, the All-Merciful, condemns men for sins which it was impossible for them to avoid, lacking grace which it was impossible for them to obtain.

Many a soul, meanwhile, wholly unable to appreciate the theological subtleties involved, was discouraged and driven back by the rigorism which these harsh views engendered in preachers and directors.

For the Faithful at large the great remedy was found in the devotion which the Jesuits everywhere preached, and the Jansenists consistently opposed, to the Sacred Heart of Jesus.

Souls, frightened and dazzled by peering into the "darkness of excessive light" which hides the mysteries of God's Predestining Grace, were taught to hide themselves from that unbearable light in the shade of Christ's sacred Humanity. We cannot fathom the counsels of God—or understand exactly what Knowledge and Will are in the Infinite God, but in Jesus Christ we see God made Man—therefore God made manifest to man; and in the mercy and compassion of the Sacred Heart, men learned to know and to love the mercy and compassion of the Eternal Word—and, therefore, of the Whole Trinity; the human created love of the Sacred Heart was the only means whereby man could realise the eternal uncreated love of the same God made Man.

XVIII. MODERNISM

NEARLY every heresy, however far-reaching its final denials, begins as an attack on one particular dogma. In the opening years of this century, however, appeared a heresy which attacked not one dogma, but the very roots of dogmatic theology.

The two sciences which made the most apparent progress during the nineteenth century were biology and textual criticism. Biology and textual criticism, therefore, were the idols of the universities and schools. To them every other science must resign precedence: by their latest results must the truth of every other department in life be judged.

This spirit not only filled the non-Catholic World, but crept among the faithful and alas! even into the priesthood.

Among the clergy ordained during the past quarter of the century were some who, finding it impossible to reconcile the dogmas of certain modern scientists with the Dogmas of the Faith, despaired not of modern science but of the Faith. Instead of holding firmly that God's revelation is infallibly true, and that all other truth must eventually be found in harmony with it, they decided that whatever in Christian doctrine was out of harmony with the spirit of the age must go—or, as they would say, be so re-interpreted as to harmonise with it.

It would seem simpler, having decided that the Church's creed was untrue, to leave the Church—this these worshippers of the Age refused to do, claiming a right to remain within the visible Church and form therein an esoteric body who, instead of moulding their beliefs to her Creed, should mould her creed to their beliefs.

Among the motives urging them to act thus two

seem to stand prominently. In the first place they were men of religious temperament and of upright life. The ideal of Our Blessed Lord stood to them for all that was most holy and most ennobling. Their sweetest remembrances, their highest aspirations and their greatest spiritual crises were all connected with, inextricably intertwined with, the thought of Catholic Sacraments, Catholic ceremonies.

They knew in the Catholic Church a sanctity realised —here more, there less—which outside her was scarcely conceived, and they wished in some way to preserve the flowers of devotion—even when they cut away the dogmas which are the very roots.

Then again, the leading Modernists were Italian or French, and the Latin races have always had a more social spirit—a keener sense of race solidarity even in spiritual things—than other races. Englishmen are naturally individualistic nonconformist, the part of "Athanasius contra mundum" is one that appeals to them, but to the Latins a man isolated, independent, is but half man. To them, the Church was the embodiment of the religious ideals and aspirations of the Western World—the storehouse of the religious experiences of their race—and to be separated from her was a religious expatriation.

They, therefore, began with the object of forming an apologetic which would appeal to the modern unscholastic mind, a restatement or rather reinterpretation of Christianity which, keeping the terms of the Creed, emptied them of all definite meaning.

In this they were helped by the philosophy accepted by those to whom they addressed themselves. The scholastic philosopher and the plain man have always agreed in holding that we are real beings in a real world capable of being known by us. They also agree in holding that there are certain truths which are in no sense contingent or possible of alteration, but are eternal and necessary, so that their opposite is inconceivable and in the strictest sense impossible. Among such truths are, "That a thing cannot, in the same sense, be and not be at the same time." "That every effect must have a cause." "That no change can take place unless brought about by an agent distinct from the thing changing." The philosophies fashionable during the eighteenth and nineteenth centuries, however, were utterly at variance with these principles.

They taught that man's intellect was able only to know appearances or phenomena, and was utterly unable to grasp reality, or indeed to pronounce whether reality *be* at all, and that the truths which man considered necessary were but necessary for him—modes in which his intellect must work as bodies must occupy space, and impossible of verification beyond that sphere of phenomena to which he is inevitably confined.

Such a philosophy served well the religious system proposed by the Modernists. Let the intellect of man, they said, confine itself to its own domain—the phenomenal universe; let it not attempt to climb, by the created to the Creator—such a road is forever impassable, but in its own sphere let it be supreme. Let no religious or metaphysical dogma stand in the way of any conclusion in physical science or history.

Do not, however, they said, imagine that Religion will lose by being thus denied any influence in the intellectual world. True, indeed, that the intellect is altogether powerless in the superphysical order—but man has within him another faculty which can reach to Religious truth not by the senses and intellect, but directly. This faculty is faith, which is on one side an appetite or desire for the Supreme Reality which is God; on the other, a direct spiritual experience thereof.

This mystic experience we try to express, but in expressing are forced to fit into intellectual forms dogmas which, being an attempt to express the inexpressible, are inevitably inadequate and so likely to mislead.

Dogmas must exist, since only in intellectual forms can experience be transmitted to others, but they are but symbols and do not express the truth experienced but rather some man's or men's reaction thereto, or, in their own phraseology, some aspect of truth. This system allowed its exponents, while professing belief in Christ, to deny any other than a symbolic truth to any article of the Creed concerning Him. His Virgin Birth, His Resurrection were declared, as phenomenal facts, to belong not to Religion but to History, and as such to be judged, approved or condemned, while as dogmas they were true with the truth of symbols.

The Scriptures were declared to fall under the same laws, to be judged by precisely the same canons as other literature—though they had a certain peculiar value as containing the religious experience of the greatest religious geniuses we know of. Sacraments, again, the modernist held to be not rites instituted by Christ, but symbolic ceremonies which the Church had found to be expressive of, and in some sense the vehicle of, spiritual experiences. It was only by degrees that the rulers of the Church awoke to the urgency of the Modernist peril. The work of the Church through the ages is to present the unchanging Faith to the changing generations. Each generation, as each race, has its own language, its own mode of thought. Hence the need for apologists knowing well both the divine science and the modern mind, able to interpret from the consecrated terminology into modern language. So for a time, although the faithful were startled and alarmed by unusual language or unlooked for concessions to the critic, yet knowing the difficulties of modern apologists and trusting to their apparent zeal and goodwill, hoped for the best, and gave the writers the benefit of the doubt as long as doubt existed. Emboldened by this leniency, the Modernists spoke out more boldly, and the Supreme Teaching Authority was aroused. Bishops wrote Pastorals denouncing the heresy and at length Rome intervened. In the Syllabus *Lamentabili* and the Encyclical *Pascendi* the various and elusive heresies and errors of "Modernism" were described and condemned. Space will not allow their full enumeration here, but among the principal were these:—

The denial of the validity of the proof of God's existence by reasoning from effect to cause, e.g. from Creation to Creator, from miracle to Revealer.

The substitution in the definition of "Faith" of a special religious faculty, sense or sentiment, for the act of the intellect, moved by the Will enabled by Grace.

The denial of the direct institution by Jesus Christ of the teaching Church and of the seven Sacraments.

The Decree and Encyclical were published in July and September of 1907. Owing, however, to the Modernist habit of using Catholic terms as a kind of cypher to express their own heresy, it was very difficult to expose and expel all the heretics. In 1910, therefore, a further vigorous measure was carried out. An anti-modernist oath of the strongest type couched in almost unevadable terms was drawn up in Rome, and, by the order of the Holy Father, every ordinand, every newly-appointed Religious Superior, all the Officials of Roman Congregations, every new preacher, confessor—in short, every cleric before entering on any new office or taking up any new responsibility, direct or indirect, for souls, was compelled to sign it.

These measures were followed by the excommunication of the leading modernists. There was, of course, the usual outcry of "tyranny, obscurantism, bigotry," from the non-Catholic world. Every journal professing rigid adherence to the "three historic Creeds" hastened in their hatred of Rome to condone the offence of those whom Rome condemned for undermining all Creeds.

Yet even in this heresy the latest and the worst the Church has ever faced, its great danger lay in the fact that its most far-reaching error was a perverted truth. No religious dogma, they said, and said truly, can adequately expressed religious truth. All dogmas involve the idea of God, and all, especially those concerning the Divine Nature, must be inadequate since He is infinite and incomprehensible.

Had they said "inadequate" only they would have expressed a truth which theologian and mystic alike have reiterated through the ages; even their phrase "dogmas are only symbols" might have passed had they remembered that a symbol must be true, or it does not symbolise. Every Revelation of God must be inadequate since He is Infinite, and both the receiving mind and the idea in which the Revelation is conveyed are finite. Even in the Beatific Vision of Heaven, we shall see the Whole but not wholly or we should be the whole. He ever remains Incomprehensible. The falsehood lay in confusing the terms "true" and "adequate."

A map is a true but inadequate representation of a country. It is not the country—but it is a true representation—and a sketch map is as true *"as far as it goes"* as the most highly detailed map. The detailed map is not *more true*, though it shows *more truth*. Again, however inadequate it is, it will not become more adequate by alteration or denial; it will only become less true; to draw the map of England as a plain oblong on the ground that the outline of capes or bays was inadequate, would be no service to geography or to tourists.

Twenty years have passed, and looking back we see the peril we escaped. We see it yet more clearly if we look round. In the Catholic Church, true to the dogmatic principle taught by the living Voice, Modernism could retain no foothold. Outside the Unity it was far otherwise: in all the sects, but especially in the Anglican Establishment, owing to her boast of comprehensiveness, and to her purposely ambiguous formulas, modernism has triumphed. One by one the old creeds, the old doctrines are restated, re-interpreted, rejected. To-day there is no sect in Europe of any size or standing that dares insist on the acceptance of any dogma whatever—in its literal meaning—as a condition of membership or even of ministry. The Catholic Church alone stands to-day as she has ever stood, *Judging*—not judged by—modern thought, rejecting in this twentieth century, as she rejected in the first or the thirteenth, every conclusion contrary to the Divine Revelation committed to her, able to weigh, assimilate and in due time *use* all the truth the age or any future age can bring—to elucidate and develop her teaching of that Revelation.

APPENDIX

SOME LESSER HERESIES

PRISCILLIANISM — ADOPTIONISM — WYCLIF — HUSS —QUIETISM — THE ILLUMINATI — FIDEISM — GALLICANISM—OLD CATHOLICS.

PRISCILLIANISM.

Priscillianism arose in Spain toward the close of the fourth century, but although Spain was apparently its birthplace, its tenets prove it of Eastern origin—as these are but a variation on old Gnostic themes. As usual we have the two kingdoms—Light (i.e. Spirit) against Darkness (i.e. Matter), the imprisonment of spirit in flesh and its redemption by means of a pseudo-incarnation of a higher being. The heresy takes its name, not from its founder—Marcus—but from his first and most prominent follower, Priscillian.

After some years of confused striving, Priscillian appealed to the Emperor who tried the case by the Prefect Erodius, with the result that, despite the intercession of St. Martin, who was horrified at spiritual offences being punished with temporal weapons, Priscillian and his leading followers were put to the sword. This, far from quelling, rather augmented the error. A quarrel arose as to the lawfulness of punishing heretics by the sword. Bishops who disapproved refused to communicate with those who upheld it—while Priscillianism spread yet further. Two more Councils were necessary before the heresy was finally overcome, the last no earlier than 563.

ADOPTIONISM.

This was a modified form of Nestorianism taught chiefly by Elipandus, bishop of Toledo, and Felix, Bishop of Urzel.

They held that while Christ was, according to His Divine Nature, the natural Son of God, according to His human Nature, He was only the adopted Son as other men are—though, of course, in the highest degree. So abstruse a point of doctrine would seem ill-fitted for popularisation, yet it spread rapidly through Western Europe and had to be discussed and condemned by four local Councils—Narbonne 788, Ratisbonne 792, Frankfort 794, and Aix-la-Chapelle 799. Pope Adrian authoritatively condemned this heresy in two epistles, one to the bishops in 785, and one to the emperor in 794. Abelard and a few later theologians held a theory bordering on this heresy, namely that while Christ, as God-made-man, is the One Only-begotten Son of God, yet by reason of His true human nature, He is the adopted Son of God *also*.

This no less than the full-fledged heresy shows a confusion in thought of Nature and Person.

Firstly, Adoption demands not simply a Nature but a Person.

Secondly, "To adopt," means to receive a stranger as a son with a son's rights. Therefore, since in Christ there is no human person but only the Divine Person of God the Son, there remains no person who could be adopted and no room in Christ for an adopted sonship in addition to His Eternal Sonship.

WYCLIF.

Lollardy took its rise from the teaching of John Wyclif, a fourteenth-century divine of Oxford, and in his latter

G

years Rector of Lutterworth. He first gained public fame as the supporter of the wealthy nobles in their attacks on the Church and clerical privileges. He justified their proceedings on the ground that all ownership and jurisdiction—or, as he said, all Dominion—being in any true sense God's alone, and Man's Dominion being a trust from Him—it followed that when a man was traitor to God by mortal sin God re-called his trust. Hence, he proceeded to say, the State has the right to take away any goods held by sinful clerics.

These opinions—however dangerous, since they gave a useful and ever-ready handle for despoilers of the Church —might have passed with little stir, but in 1380 he dared to deny the doctrine of transubstantiation, and about the same time he founded a body of Poor Priests whom he sent to preach his heresies throughout England. Ecclesiastical Authority was roused in defence of the Faith. Oxford condemned his Eucharistic Heresy in 1381—and at a meeting convoked at Blackfriars in the following year twenty-four propositions from his writings were condemned. No very vigorous measures, however, were taken against him personally, and he died at peace in his own rectory in 1384 at the age of sixty. Meanwhile his preachers spread, especially in London and in the Eastern Counties, his manifold errors. Their teachings varied from year to year and place to place, but were chiefly: the sole authority of Scripture; the pre-eminence of Preaching over Liturgy or Sacraments; the denial of the Mass and of the Invocation of Saints. For a century the danger was recurrent. Indeed, it had not wholly died out at the time of the Reformation.

Huss.

In England the Church more than held its own against Wyclif, but in Bohemia his greatest follower, Huss, not only corrupted the Bohemian Church but caused a civil war. Huss, the rector of the University of Prague, imported and translated the writings of Wyclif and preached his doctrines from the pulpit. In spite of Papal condemnations, he still upheld the false teaching, and at the advice of Sigismond, the emperor, ventured to appear before the Council of Constance and defend them there. He was condemned and in the year 1415 burnt at Constance. This condemnation the Bohemians took as a national insult. Over four hundred nobles signed a manifesto denying the existence of heresy in Bohemia. They defended heretical preachers from ecclesiastical discipline and allowed the new teaching to run riot. The great cry of the Schismatics was for communion in both kinds. Hence their name *Utraquists*. Not content with preaching they spread their doctrines by force. Beginning with an irregular and inordinate devotion to the Blessed Sacrament, they ended by denying it altogether, and with it nearly every other Christian doctrine. They split into sects which fought —literally—not only with the orthodox but between themselves until the whole country was a welter of blood and impiety.

The Church finally made some disciplinary concessions to the moderate party and so gained their allegiance against the extremists: but it was many many years before the trouble finally died out.

Quietism.

Just as Christian asceticism was aped by an asceticism springing from Manichean principles—so Christian mysticism was endangered by counterfeits tainted with Pantheistic errors. The most pernicious of these errors appear in the Quietist system set out by Michael Molinos

—a popular director in Rome during the latter part of the seventeenth century.

He taught that perfection lay not in training and supernaturalising, but in quelling, and as far as possible annihilating our natural powers. We should, he taught, be absolutely passive, that God may do with us what He wills. Exterior good works are useless for sanctification, nor are spiritual acts any more pleasing in God's sight. We should not try to practise virtue, nor even to avoid vice; sensible devotion also was but a spiritual defilement, and love of the saints, of our Lady or even of the Sacred Humanity itself, was useless or evil since these are sensible objects. Abnegation of self, he taught, should go so far that the perfect should even be indifferent to their own salvation—nay, more, to the behaviour of their own flesh—sensual sin, he declared, being no hindrance to perfection as long as the soul remained undisturbed in its quiet. The Pope condemned Molinos' whole system in 1687, and Molinos was publicly condemned to penance at the command of the Holy Office.

While these immoral extremes disgusted all decent-minded people, there was in the main Quietist tenets—the doctrine of Perfect Indifference and of Pure Love of God—a certain fascination for generous souls. These less gross parts of Molinos' heresy found entrance into France, especially through the writings of the fervent, but misguided, Madame Guyon. Some ecclesiastics becoming suspicious of her teaching, a group of divines met at Issy and examined and condemned her writings. In her fall was involved one much greater than herself. Fénelon, the great Bishop of Cambrai, a man renowned for his holy life, and the tutor of the Dauphin, was among the friends of Madame Guyon. On being asked to join in her condemnation, he rather defended her, and wrote, in explanation of his doctrine on the spiritual life, the well-known *Maxims of the Saints*. A veritable war of controversy rose against it and Fénelon appealed to Rome. Two years were occupied in examining the book, but judgment was eventually pronounced against it, and Fénelon loyally submitted.

His system was a modified form of Molinos'. It pushed the practice of disinterested love of God so far as to make the virtue of Hope, and the Love arising therefrom an imperfection to be outgrown by the soul as it advances in perfection. Again, he adopts various sayings of contemplative saints on the passivity of the soul under God's hand in certain miraculous states of prayer and proposes them as a rule of ordinary prayer and charity. Fénelon made a most generous act of submission—recanting every sentiment contrary to the teaching of the Church.

The pantheistic tendencies of these pseudo-mystics, however, so alarmed the authorities that true mysticism also fell under suspicion, and for more than two centuries spiritual writers were inclined to confine the faithful to vocal prayer and discursive meditation, all desire for contemplative prayer being treated as an unholy ambition likely to lead the soul to some form of Quietism or even Pantheism.

The Illuminati.

The story of the "Illuminati" founded by Adam Weishaupt, reads like a burlesque of the Protestant conception of the Society of Jesus. Its founder, Adam Weishaupt, was an ex-pupil of the Jesuits and a professor, first of Civil and afterwards, in 1772–3, of Canon Law at the University of Ingoldstadt. Imbibing the fashionable rationalism of his time, he sought a means for spreading naturalism or deism throughout Europe.

With the aid of Freis von Knigge, a Freemason, he founded an inner circle within Freemasonry. The members of this, called the Illuminati, formed a Society pledged to introduce their founder's views in every rank of life and thus destroy all revealed religion. Many Freemasons were enrolled including Ferdinand, Duke of Brunswick, but the objects of the Society leaked out and Church and State were alike alarmed. Rulers declared it illegal, and the Pope exposed and condemned it in 1785. Weishaupt, himself, gradually modified his views as he advanced in years and was reconciled to the Church before his death in 1830.

FIDEISM (Traditionalism).

Fideism and Traditionalism are names given to various systems of thought which, accepting the despair of the Intellect into which modern systems of Philosophy fall, try to account for man's knowledge of the primary truths of Religion. All truth, they said, and the first conditions and instruments of knowledge such as language, were the immediate gift of God to our first Parents, whence we derive them by an unbroken tradition. Our knowledge of God, of Virtue, of all rational principles are thus obtained by faith, not reasoning.

Meant, as these theories were, to protect Religion from Rationalism, they are a treacherous defence—more dangerous than the attack. Although their propagators, of whom the brilliant de Lamennais is the most famous, desired to serve the Church by finding an apologetic less distasteful to their age than the old scholastic argument, yet the Church, ever the champion of Reason in its own sphere, condemned the thesis. From time to time one or other proposition involving these theories was condemned, and at last the Vatican Council in 1870 solemnly defined that "The one true God and Lord can be known with certainty from the things that are made."

GALLICANISM.

The Church has always claimed to be the Messenger from God; the Infallible Guardian of Christ's Revelation. She has always taught, moreover, that the Pope as successor of St. Peter is the Supreme Pastor over the whole Flock—Christ's Vicar upon earth. The *exact* relation between these two truths, however, was left undefined.

In France and the countries on her eastern borders a school of thought arose which minimised the Papal prerogatives in the interest of the State. Nominally it stood also for the dignity and independence of bishops and Councils, but as usual independence of the Pope means for bishops dependence on the State.

This *Gallican* School held (1) that the Pope's definitions were not Infallible in *themselves* but only after acceptance by the Universal Church; (2) that a General Council's authority was above that of a Pope. Some French ecclesiastics also claimed that the king had the right to forbid the publication in France of Papal Bulls, that no act done by the king's agent on his authority could involve excommunication, and that the king could prevent any bishop's recourse to Rome even if the Pope commanded his presence.

In opposition to this disloyal minimising school another party went to the opposite extreme and in its zeal for Catholic Unity stretched Papal prerogatives so far that scarcely any room was left for Political and National Liberty, for Episcopal Jurisdiction, or for Theological Study. While this controversy was at its height the Vatican Council met in 1870. Against those who minimised the Papal claims, it defined that the

Pope is gifted with that Infallibility with which Christ willed His Church should be endowed; while contrary to the wishes of those who exaggerated the Council's definition, it declared this Infallibility limited to those occasions when the Pope (1) speaks as Supreme Teacher; (2) defines a doctrine of Faith or Morals; (3) declares the definition binding on all the Faithful.

THE OLD CATHOLICS.

This decision while it was received with joy by the vast majority of the Faithful was extremely unwelcome to a group of Liberal or minimising Catholics, among whom certain German theologians were particularly prominent. About fourteen thousand met in Germany in the September following the definition and repudiated it.

Döllinger, Professor of Canon Law and Church History at Munich, and a famous writer on Church history and the history of dogma, also wrote and spoke against it. He and his brother were excommunicated and in the following year all the malcontents gathered together to form what is known as the Old Catholic Church, which gained episcopal orders from a Dutch Jansenist bishop. Its principle tenets were, firstly, *Erastianism:* that is (a) the choice of the State rather than the Universal Church as the centre of religious authority; (b) participation of the Laity in Church government.

Secondly, repudiation of every dogma not in harmony with the actual consciousness of the Church.

In this second principle we seem to see an anticipation of a leading Modernist principle.

The Old Catholics were warmly supported both in Germany and Switzerland by the State, which hoped that new national Churches might be more amenable to State dominion than the Church in union with the Holy

See. In spite of all State encouragement, however, the new Church soon dwindled almost away. It allied itself with any and every heresy. As we saw above its first bishop was consecrated by a Jansenist. It lost, one by one, practically every Catholic doctrine and practice. In the countries of its origin it is now practically Protestant.

INDEX

108   *Index*